Advance Praise for *All In*

"Working fathers and mothers need the same things: paid leave, flexible work, child care, and access to services that allow them to be who they want to be at work, at home, and in the community. *All In* does a superb job of showing how we can make positive changes that benefit organizations, employees and their families, and our society."

> —Stewart D. Friedman, founder of the Wharton
> Work/Life Integration Project and author of
> *Leading the Life You Want*

"*All In* is at once a reality check and a passionate call to action. The changes we need in the workplace—from paid parental leave to additional flexibility and more—will not only be better for families, they'll also be better for business. Josh Levs lays out a clear and compelling path for how dads can join with moms to make these changes happen."

> —Jen Dulski, president and COO of Change.org

"Josh Levs leaves virtually no stone unturned in cataloging the state of modern fatherhood, uncovering its game-changing impact on masculinity, relationships, media, marketing, and more. His insights and conclusions will serve as a road map to the coming decade of parenting and relationship research, family leave policies, and product marketing efforts."

> —John Pacini, cofounder of XY Media and
> Dad 2.0 Summit

"One of the most important books written about fatherhood. Engaging and entertaining, *All In* should be read by fathers, mothers, CEOs, policy makers, and anyone who cares about improving American society."

—Cynthia Calvert, president of Workforce 21C

"*All In* represents the voice of any parent who feels boxed in by gender stereotypes, at home *and* at the office. Josh's energetic style and exhaustive research—from hundreds of real parents navigating really challenging times—comprise an important treatise on how to reboot our obsolete instincts and policies toward working parents.

—Doug French, cofounder of XY Media and Dad 2.0 Summit

All
in

All in

How Our Work-First Culture Fails Dads, Families, and Businesses—And How We Can Fix It Together

JOSH LEVS

HarperOne
An Imprint of HarperCollinsPublishers

HarperOne

Identifying details of certain individuals have been changed to protect their privacy.

HarperCollins books may be purchased for educational, business, or sales promotional use. For information please e-mail the Special Markets Department at SPsales@harpercollins.com.

HarperCollins website: http://www.harpercollins.com

HarperCollins®, 📖®, and HarperOne™ are trademarks of HarperCollins Publishers.

FIRST EDITION

Library of Congress Cataloging-in-Publication Data

Levs, Josh.
 All in : how our work-first culture fails dads, families, and businesses—and how we can fix it together / Josh Levs. — First edition.
    pages cm
 Includes bibliographical references.
 ISBN 978–0–06–234961–3
 1. Work and family—United States. 2. Father and child—United States.
 3. Families—United States. 4. Parental leave—United States. I. Title.
 HD4904.25.L476   2015
 306.3—dc23   2014042031

15 16 17 18 19 RRD(H) 10 9 8 7 6 5 4 3 2 1

To M, who opened me to love and is the ultimate partner on the ultimate journey; and to R, J, and A, each a Big Bang of your own, the loves of our life.

Contents

Part III. Fixing Pop Culture

Part IV. Fatherlessness

Part V. Sex

Part VI. The All-In Life

Introduction

It starts the second our kids are born. We join the revolution that is reshaping parenting in America. The roles of moms and dads have stretched out, becoming busier, more varied, and more complex than ever before. Men and women are sharing child rearing and household responsibilities, supporting each other's careers, making financial decisions together, and building futures as partners. We're engaged in all aspects of family life.

"Dads are not down the hall with a pipe in their mouth, the Don Draper type, like my father was," says Doug French, who has two sons. "My father is still freaked out that I watched both my children emerge. He can't fathom that!"

But the structures that shape our family lives remain rigid. It's an astounding disconnect. Our laws, corporate policies, and gender-based expectations in the workplace are straight out of the 1950s. And they're taking a hell of a toll, preventing us from living out the equality we believe in. Millions of stay-at-home moms want to get back to work and advance their careers. Millions of working dads want more time at home to raise their kids. But society doesn't allow it. It's boxing us in.

When dads try to take paternity leave, they're often rebuffed. When they manage to take it or pursue a flexible schedule, many get punished. Men face derision, demotions, and even loss of their jobs when they make family a priority. Women, meanwhile, often face the opposite pressure. They're punished for working full-time by bosses or coworkers who think they should be home more. "It is shocking how many policies still discriminate," says Keith Cunningham-Parmeter, one of the top attorneys fighting to end such policies. "It's like the Wild West days."

"Today's gender-discrimination polices women into caregiving roles and men out of them," says attorney Joan Williams of the Center for WorkLife Law, another leading warrior in the effort to break out of these structures. "Men are being policed into a very specific form of masculinity."

Why the disconnect? Why hasn't the corporate world kept up with American family life? Because the people in power are often oblivious to the realities of modern families. Most executives are men who acknowledge they don't make family a priority. Few women make it to the executive suites, and those who do are less likely to have children than their male counterparts. The vast majority of top executives see work-family conflicts as primarily a "women's problem," a recent—and, sadly, completely unsurprising—study found.[1]

It's a vicious cycle. People who don't have a family or make it a priority are rewarded in the workplace. They rise to positions of power. They, then, are responsible for the rules and culture.

In the pages ahead, you'll learn the story of a dad who took off just three days after his daughter was born in an emergency situation. When he returned to work, his boss rebuked him. That boss was a pregnant woman. You'll hear about the case of a lawyer who was a star at his firm until his pregnant wife attempted suicide. He took time off to be a caregiver and, when he came back, was insulted for it. He lost opportunities and was soon fired. You'll read about a teacher who decided to take two years off to care for his baby without losing his job, since his contract said any teacher could. But then his bosses said, "Oops. We only meant for that to apply to women." You'll also learn about the case of a state trooper who was refused the time off he was legally entitled to because, according to his boss, women are supposed to do the caregiving unless they are "in a coma or dead."

This isn't discrimination against men. It's discrimination against *men and women.* These one-size-fits-all presumptions take choices away. Moms end up doing more at home, dads do more at work, and the time warp of the American workplace remains alive and well. Often, moms don't even go back to work or don't get the chance to pursue professional opportunities, because their husbands aren't allowed basic flexibility.

In her book *Lean In: Women, Work, and the Will to Lead,* which launched a movement, Facebook COO Sheryl Sandberg calls on women to "lean in," to press harder to break into leadership roles and build a fulfilling professional and personal life.[2] When she and I sat down at her offices in Menlo Park, California, to speak for this book, we agreed: These structures must change so that men and women have the chance to be all in both at work and at home. "The laws are really important, so we give equal maternity and paternity leave," she said of Facebook.

It's time for corporate America to follow this and other examples, time to honor the gender equality it professes to believe in. We talk a good game about family values in this country, but our laws, policies, and stigmas prove that we don't adequately value families. And you can't value families without valuing—equally—daughters and sons, mothers and fathers.

As you'll see in this book, it isn't just good for families. It's *good for business,* and critical for advancing the American economy. The World Economic Forum traces a relationship between gender equality and a strong economy, explaining: "Countries and companies can be competitive only if they develop, attract and retain the best talent, both male and female."[3] Coming up, you'll see my proposal for taking a big leap forward by *lowering* U.S. taxes.

We can fix these problems plaguing our society. Through simple steps, we can create big solutions. As you'll see, my experience proves it.

This requires men joining hands with women in the battle—something many women have been calling for. "Why do we continue to focus on this as a women's issue, when the evidence makes it so clear that it's shared by men?" NYU sociologist Kathleen Gerson asked in a *Bloomberg Businessweek* article on the balance between work and home life.[4] Writing on similar issues in the *New Republic,* Rebecca Traister argued that women "*must* stop having these conversations amongst ourselves."[5]

Actress Emma Watson, known worldwide for having played Hermione in the Harry Potter films, took this same call and made it a global one. At the United Nations, she delivered an address announcing the program HeForShe, a "solidarity movement for gender equality." She said:

> How can we affect change in the world when only half of it
> is invited or feel welcome to participate in the conversation?
> Men—I would like to take this opportunity to extend your
> formal invitation. Gender equality is your issue too.
>
> Because to date, I've seen my father's role as a parent being
> valued less by society despite my needing his presence as a child
> as much as my mother's. I've seen young men suffering from
> mental illness unable to ask for help for fear it would make
> them look less "macho." . . . I've seen men made fragile and
> insecure by a distorted sense of what constitutes male success.
> Men don't have the benefits of equality either. We don't often
> talk about men being imprisoned by gender stereotypes, but I
> can see that that they are and that when they are free, things
> will change for women as a natural consequence.[6]

That's where this book comes in. It's the result of more than 150 hours of interviews, in which men from all walks of life open up. They divulge their struggles to find balance, and their thoughts on all the issues that play into the fight for gender equality: work, home life, money, "male privilege," "female gatekeeping," and a lot more.

"If my kids are blessed to be fathers, I want them to have an easier time making the decision about whether to stay home or stay at work," says Chad Welch, a leader of the National At-Home Dad Network. "I don't want them to have those battles."

The number of stay-at-home dads has risen dramatically.[7] Welch's network estimates it could be as many as 1.8 million men.[8] One in five dads with working wives are primary caregivers to their preschool-age children.[9]

Working dads, meanwhile, are experiencing as much work-life conflict as moms—perhaps even more, according to one study.[10] About half would rather stay home if their spouses made enough money to live on comfortably. Three-quarters want more time with their kids. Virtually all say that when considering a new job, they look into how much it would interfere with family time.[11] These conflicts are not making dads any less productive at work. But the more we commit to building deep, emotional relationships with our children, the harder these conflicts get.

"I am constantly juggling work and life issues, often from the road, and often not juggling very well," says Kipp Jarecke-Cheng, in Maplewood, New Jersey. "My work suffers because I can't fully focus or commit to my job duties because of my concerns about my family, and my family suffers because I worry about doing a good job at work. I feel as if I can't devote myself fully to either, and both end up getting half-baked attention."

He feels that his bosses and colleagues don't "have a very deep appreciation for the challenges of wanting to work hard and also have enough quality time with my family. I'm coming to the realization that if I wanted to have the kind of relationship I seek with my child, I will likely need to leave the rat race for an extended period of time."

"I'm a working dad, and I want it all," says Carter Gaddis, father of two in Lutz, Florida. "I don't even know what 'all' is, but I want a rewarding career; I want to be the father and husband that I'm supposed to be, and I want to be able to squeeze that all into a twenty-four-hour day. And, by the way, I have to sleep." Replace the words "father" and "husband" with "mother" and "wife," and it's exactly what millions of women say.

A striking quote comes from one dad in Washington, D.C., who sometimes has to travel for work. "I know I have been an imperfect father. I know I have made mistakes. I have lost count of all the times, over the years, when the demands of work have taken me from the duties of fatherhood," he said. "There were many days . . . when I felt like my family was a million miles away, and I knew I was missing moments of my daughters' lives that I'd never get back. It is a loss I will never fully accept."[12]

That dad is President Barack Obama, and the fact that he speaks out like this shows that as men in the world of hands-on parenting we have—to borrow a phrase—"come a long way." Obama has placed such a high value on evenings with his family that some political watchers call it a reason for congressional gridlock (a suggestion he rejects). He has done substantially fewer social engagements with lawmakers than his predecessors, giving up schmoozing with other Washington heavyweights in favor of hearing about what his daughters learned at school that day.

From dinner promptly at 6:30 P.M.—at which they discuss the best and worst parts of their days—through bedtime, the Obamas have worked to achieve what they call a "normal" family life. That's made the president a homebody. He even coached his daughter Sasha's basketball team.

He talks about his kids frequently in interviews, lamenting how they're "growing up so fast," something all of us parents wrestle with. "Now that my girls are getting older, they don't want to spend that much time with me," he said. "Between school, sports, social life, and their community service, they're not around as much. So that gets me teary sometimes."[13]

This change from the old stereotype—the dad who comes home from work, kicks his feet up, and reads the newspaper—has been in the making for decades. The women's liberation movement was in high gear before many of today's dads were born. We were raised by parents who drilled gender equality into our minds. We listened to *Free to Be You and Me* from before we could speak. By the time we reached adulthood, it seemed obvious: of course women are just as capable at work and men are just as capable at home.

But we didn't insist on laws and policies that make it possible for us to be equally present at home. "We were supposed to be the *Free to Be You and Me* generation, and that promise didn't come true," Sheryl Sandberg says. The biggest reason, she believes, is that "we tried to change the workforce, and we didn't change the home. And it fell apart for women. Women went into the workforce in massive numbers, but they couldn't stay in with the same dedication," because their husbands weren't doing as much at home.

The battle to change that has begun. It may be a tiny silver lining from a storm that wrecked the U.S. economy. "The 2008 recession was the nuclear event," says John Pacini, a cofounder of the Dad 2.0 Summit, an annual gathering for hundreds of fathers. "What was so transformative was that so many men were 'downsized,' while their wives were not. Suddenly, you had many more men engaging in domestic roles in the family in ways they never had before, while the women were breadwinners."

It was called the "mancession," because it disproportionately affected industries that employed mostly men, such as construction. I always rejected that term, partly because it does a disservice to the millions of women who were affected. But the number of unemployed dads who stayed home did jump to a historic high, hitting 2.2 million in 2010 (it has since slipped a bit as the economy improved).[14]

"It's great. It's fun stuff," K. J. Copeland told me for a CNN story.

He was a corporate recruiter who lost his job and became a stay-at-home dad. Though he loved it, he also learned what millions of moms already knew: "It's a grind. . . . Every minute of the day, it's all about you. Everybody wants something from you. There's no quiet time."[15]

Copeland was one of several men gathered for a TV story on how the economy was affecting fatherhood. I was covering the recession, anchoring the "CNN Stimulus Desk," which probed where billions of government dollars were going. I was also, at that point, the father of a two-year-old boy who had had major heart surgery at birth. As sole provider amid rising unemployment, I had the same worries as many other dads. Studies showed men were putting in more hours at the office, and bringing more work home.[16] "When you're a one-income family, and you have three mouths depending on you, it's a lot of stress," said Joe Cerone, a dad on the panel.

I asked the working fathers in the group whether they were ever jealous of the stay-at-home parent. "Yes. Just the amount of time that she's able to spend with my daughters, and the bond that they seem to have," said Lee May, a father of two and a commissioner for DeKalb County, Georgia.

"You're told a lot about the first things that they've done," added Cerone, a marketing executive raising a daughter with his male partner. "Like, just this morning, when he dropped her off at school, she said something the first time that she's never said before. And I missed out on it, because I was at work."

As parents, we know that feeling. I hate that feeling. From the time I became a father, I tried to organize my life so I'd be home as much as possible. I pitched a new role to the president of CNN, in which I'd report mostly from our headquarters in Atlanta. That allowed me to avoid the typical track of becoming a correspondent who travels all the time. A colleague who always travels told me he feels his kids "barely know" him.

Still, there have been times that my work kept me out of the house for incredible hours, especially in the early days of the recession. The financial incentive was there—the more I worked, the more I got paid. While shooting a pilot, I flew back and forth between New York and Atlanta so often that I'd have to look around the room for a few seconds each morning to remember which city I was in. On the days I realized I wasn't home, I'd feel that familiar pang in my gut.

Interviewing this group of dads, I saw that they—just like millions of others all over the world—shared my commitment to "dadhood." After each segment aired, those of us at the anchor desk chatted about it on air. A colleague asked me what the number one piece of advice I took away from the conversation was.

"What's really interesting to me is no matter how much they work, or whether they're out of work, the one thing that they all agree on ultimately is that there's no question what's most important in this world: passing on values to their kids," I answered. "And whether they only get that little bit of time or they get a lot of time, packing it with quality. I know this sounds trite, but the truth is they have to make active efforts every day."

The reactions to these reports blew me away. I heard from many viewers as well as colleagues with the same message: they'd never seen anything like it. The web page that contained videos of these segments became the most popular page on the CNN Newsroom blog. I even heard from other members of the media fascinated by the idea that I, a dad in the media, was interviewing fellow fathers.

Talking with a group of dads about these issues seemed so obvious to me. But to others, it wasn't. That's when I realized no one else was doing this. In mainstream media, "mom panels" were common, and "parenting" subjects almost always involved only moms or a group of moms with a token dad.

Dads needed a bigger voice. I decided to try to provide one. So along with reporting on the biggest news stories, I became CNN's "dad columnist" and the "resident dad" on the parenting show *Raising America,* which aired on CNN's sister network HLN.

From this new vantage point, I saw how misrepresented and mis-understood fathers were in the mainstream. A case in point was a ri-diculous, offensive column that was carried front and center on CNN .com—on Father's Day no less—telling dads to "wake the hell up." The piece, which contained no facts or statistics, was from a stay-at-home father complaining that "most" dads "just wanna chill in front of SportsCenter with a bowl of chips" when they get home, "have no problem with passing the tykes off for more alone time with mom," and "have no remote idea" how hard their stay-at-home wives are working.[17]

The vast majority of today's dads actually embody the opposite of that stereotype. But it's so prevalent that even some of them believe it. "People have a hard time letting go of this idea," says Chris Routly, a leader in the army of dad bloggers battling this false impression—particularly in television shows and ads, a phenomenon we'll explore in this book. "People internalize these portrayals. Dads are considered a 'safe target.' And as long as fatherhood is mocked freely, fathers will continue to be looked at as secondary parents. Dad is like a footnote."

This sexism damages America. It tells people in power that their presumptions about gender roles are right. But it also does something even more insidious: it drives a wedge between men and women. It creates a false gender war, pitting us against each other. The stereo-type sends the message that things would be better if only men would take responsibility at home instead of being so lazy and indifferent. It angers men who feel insulted and discounted. It also plagues custody cases and exacerbates the fatherlessness crisis, which we'll explore in subsequent chapters.

At CNN I've been called "Truth Seeker in Chief" and "Mr. Re-ality," because I love fact-checking. I did a lot of that for this book. Here, now, are some critical truths about modern parents.

Today's dads and moms work equally hard on behalf of their families. When you combine paid work with household chores and child care, they put in just about the same amount of time. And we're talking a lot of hours. On average, dads put in about fifty-four hours of work time to moms' fifty-three.[18] In two-income homes, moms work fifty-nine hours to dads' fifty-eight.[19] In single-income homes, the breadwinner works more overall.[20] And although the number of female breadwinners is on the rise, dads are still the vast majority of primary or sole breadwinners.[21]

Working dads who live with their children spend an average of three hours a day with them.[22] Eighty-one percent play with their kids every day. Virtually all the rest play with their kids at least several times a week. Virtually all bathe, diaper, dress, and eat with their kids just as often. Two-thirds talk with their kids about their day every day. Six in ten read to their kids every day or at least several times a week.[23] One study found that eight in ten dads report changing diapers just as often or even more often than their wives while they're home. The moms polled said they change diapers more often, but didn't say the dads aren't doing the duty.[24]

Dads do twice as much cooking and cleaning as their fathers did, though still not as much as moms.[25] But this fact often gets taken out of context to create an unfair picture. One claim that gets floated around is that women do much more housework even when both parents work "full-time." Here's the problem with that. "Full-time" in these studies is defined as working at least thirty hours a week. Men in dual-income couples work outside the home an average of forty-two hours a week; women, thirty-one hours.[26] "Spending eleven fewer hours at home and with the kids doesn't mean working dads are freeloaders any more than spending eleven fewer hours at work makes working moms slackers," writes Richard Dorment, *Esquire* senior editor, in an article called "Why Men Still Can't Have It All."[27]

Another example is the so-called leisure gap. Some people say dads get more leisure time, and I can't blame them. A study did say that "in America, fathers, on average, have about three hours more leisure time per week than mothers."[28] But when I looked at the actual numbers, here's what I found: moms report spending a bit less time each day on "leisure and sports," but they also report spending a bit more time on sleeping and other "personal care."[29] The differences are in the same range. So, for example, a mom goes to bed while a dad spends twenty minutes watching TV, then goes to bed, and they both get up at the same time. One doesn't get "more" than the other; they just used that little bit of time differently.

I'd never write a story that declares simply, "Moms Get More Sleep," because that would be equally misleading. One story from a popular news website carried the headline "Women Lazier Than Men, Global Survey Finds."[30] The survey actually found that "in most countries inactivity is higher in women than in men."[31] Numerous issues contribute to this, including access to sports and the fact that men are more often involved in physical labor.

I could fill this entire book with reality checks, but the point is simple: overall, modern parents in the United States are working hard and doing their best. It's the era of all-in parenting. And, by and large, neither gender is letting the other down. It's similar in many countries, particularly those in the Organization for Economic Cooperation and Development.[32]

Moms are like Elastigirl, the superhero from *The Incredibles* who could reach out for miles and contort into any position to take care of her family and simultaneously save the world. Dads are like Stretch Armstrong, a toy we used to have as kids. You could pull his arms until they reached a span of a couple feet. The commercials cheered, "He bends! He stretches! You can even tie him in knots!" What parent doesn't feel that way? Also like Elastigirl and Stretch Armstrong, parents are expected to look amazing and have perfect bodies along the way. (A shirtless magazine-model dad will give us a reality check on that, ahead.) We're not superheroes, but we're doing our best.

Beth and Carter Gaddis exemplify this. They get up together each morning. Carter wakes up one of the boys, while Beth wakes the other. "Carter makes lunch," Beth says. "Carter leaves to go to work. Then I leave and drop off the kids at 7:20. Then he leaves work at 5:15 to pick them up from day care. I leave work half an hour later. By the time I get home, Carter usually has dinner ready."

"Who does the household chores?" I ask.

"Beth does most of them, because I'm utterly lazy and useless," Carter says, semi-joking.

"Wait—you make dinner every night!" I interject.

"He's a better cook," Beth says, smiling. Carter also does the yard work. Beth does the cleaning and laundry.

Another couple who split responsibilities, Stevie and John Kinnear of Salt Lake City, say, "We tag team it."

"John's not trusted with the laundry," Stevie adds with a smile. "But to be fair, I'm not trusted to cook."

"On a typical day," Stevie says, "we come home, and I kind of entertain our two kids while John makes dinner. And then we'll both clean up. We'll both play with the kids. And then, one thing that actually surprises a lot of people is we take turns putting the kids to bed. On the weekends, we both have things we want to do—go for a run or take a nap. We let each other do those things. It's actually pretty even."

Richard Dorment, the *Esquire* editor, says his wife, a lawyer, "really works the hardest (professionally) between the two of us. At home, she thinks she does more than I do, and I think I do more than she does. It's the conversation that's been happening in some form for millennia.

"The other night, she was closing a deal and literally was up the entire night. At 6:00 she got up from her desk to go feed the baby. I was up with our son, who's three, making breakfast and getting him ready for school. Our sitter came and took over with the baby, and we both went to work. We came home, she crashed, I gave the kids baths and dinner, and we both went to sleep. We just sort of balance out each other's professional needs."

This kind of balance is typical, particularly for today's young couples, says Brad Harrington, executive director of the Boston College Center for Work and Family. "These parents think, 'It's not a question of whether I will be involved; it's a question of how do we divide the responsibility.' That's become more the reality. This is something organizations have to talk about, because that's how the country works."

Not every family seeks a fifty-fifty breakdown of responsibilities at home. Lara lives in Marietta, Georgia, and spends each day entertaining three-year-old Ben. They color, build with blocks, go for walks, and work on potty training. While Ben naps, there's mopping, scrubbing, and vacuuming to be done. Still, Lara manages to stay in shape by squeezing in exercise time with kettlebells and a stair climber. In the evening, Lara cooks dinner and cleans everything up—even though at that point both parents are home.

Lara is his last name. His first name is Nick. He's a stay-at-home dad. "I feel, since I'm home, there is no reason for my wife to do anything but just relax when she comes home from work and spend time with our family," he says. That doesn't mean she is sitting with her feet up, though. After work she rolls her sleeves up and plays with Ben.

If this division of labor works for the Laras, a similar division might work for another family in which the dad brings home the income and the mom handles most household chores. That's not inherently a bad thing. What's bad is not being able to make the choice.

And that brings us back to the need to eradicate our backward laws, policies, and gender expectations. It's something President Obama has personally called for. "A mother deserves a day off to care for a sick child or sick parent without running into hardship. And you know what? A father does too," he said in his 2014 State of the Union address. "It is time to do away with workplace policies that belong in a *Mad Men* episode."

For the first time in years, I wasn't watching the State of the Union live or reporting on it. My wife and I were getting the kids to bed. As soon as the president made those remarks, my phone started going wild with every kind of beep and alert it has. Calls, e-mails, texts, tweets, Facebook posts, and LinkedIn messages were flocking in, saying, "The president just spoke about you!" Of course, he didn't. But at the time, I had suddenly found myself in a new spotlight, as the "poster boy" in the fight for sensible paternity leave.[33]

Months earlier, my wife and I found out she was pregnant with a girl. We were thrilled. We had two boys by then. Each had arrived with fanfare and drama. The first, as I mentioned, had heart surgery and, thankfully, came through it perfectly healthy. The second was born into my arms on the floor of our bedroom when he and my wife conspired to skip labor altogether. (Birth is the most astounding thing there is, and I'm in awe of and grateful to every woman, especially my wife, who chooses to go through it.) With our daughter, we were hoping to finally have a drama-free birth. But having a child is like going all in in poker, and you never know what cards you'll be dealt.

We decided that I would need to be home after the baby's birth. I was looking forward to it. But there seemed to be an oversight in the benefits that Time Warner, the parent company of CNN, provided. As the rules were written, virtually any parent had the option of ten paid weeks of leave after the arrival of a new baby. Biological moms got this, and so did moms or dads who would care for a child who joined the family through surrogacy or adoption. But there was one exception: a man could not get those weeks for his own biological child born to the child's biological mother.

Yes, it's as strange as it sounds. If my baby was from some other guy's sperm and I legally adopted the child, I would get the ten paid weeks. If a surrogate carried the baby, I'd get the time. If I put my baby up for adoption, and some other guy at Time Warner adopted her, that guy could get ten paid weeks. But not me.

It gets even more ridiculous. Time Warner gave ten paid weeks to some people who were not legally parents. If someone adopted a child, and that person's same-sex domestic partner worked for Time Warner, that employee got the ten paid weeks to care for the child even without co-adopting the child.

If you need to read the three paragraphs above again to make sense of them, I don't blame you. It takes a color-coded flowchart to understand how Time Warner made it possible for all sorts of parents, and some people who were not legally parents, to get ten paid weeks while denying the option only to men who had kids the traditional way. Even if, heaven forbid, a man's wife died in childbirth, the policy still did not allow him the same ten paid weeks to be caregiver to his biological child.

To be clear, I was fully in support of all these people getting ten paid weeks. The problem was excluding dads like me from having the same option. Under the policy, I could get only two paid weeks. So I inquired about the process of challenging a benefit rule and followed the protocol. I went straight to the Benefits department within Human Resources. I was told that, apparently, no other dad or dad-to-be inside CNN had raised this point before. Some guys later told me they had wanted to challenge the rule, but were afraid to or didn't know they had the right.

Benefits asked me to put the request in writing. So in an e-mail, I explained that the policies

> seemed to be the result of an effort to be inclusive and fair when
> it comes to providing benefits for employees who have children.
> Unfortunately, out of the best intentions, our company cur-
> rently excludes one absolutely critical, growing minority group
> for an important benefit. The net effect is that the company
> penalizes my family. . . . It's also outdated, now that many men
> fulfill these critical roles at home. Why should another parent
> be allowed ten weeks of full pay to do so, but not me? Why do I
> receive only one-fifth of that benefit?

No one challenged my argument. My attorneys, whom I consulted each step of the way, were confident the company would grant my request. Court precedent was on my side, and companies don't want this kind of legal hassle, they said. But they and I underestimated the obstinacy we'd run into.

Over the following weeks, I asked frequently for a response, because my wife and I needed to plan. I kept getting no answer. At one point, Benefits informed me that the conversations, which involved all the companies within Time Warner, were going in a way that seemed as though they could bring good news. But still, no answer.

Then the Levs family penchant for birth drama struck again. My wife went in for her thirty-five-week appointment, and doctors discovered she had severe symptoms of preeclampsia. She was immediately put to bed, with magnesium running through an IV to combat the high blood pressure. That night, they induced, kicking off a painful twenty-four-hour period. Her strength shone through yet again. During this time, I again alerted work, hoping for an answer. Still, none.

Our daughter joined us that night after another heroic delivery by my wife. Fortunately, our daughter's health was great. She came out kicking and screaming—unlike with our second son, who had showed no signs of life for more than a minute when he was born into my arms. Our daughter was spry and energetic, though tiny enough to fit easily in one hand.

A few days later, she and my wife came home. Our whole family was already in love with our baby girl. I was taking care of everyone as best I could, but still no answer from work, no matter how many times I asked. Caring for my wife, baby, and two sons, I was burning through the two weeks quickly. Finally, eleven days after the birth, I explained to Benefits that I had to tell my work team whether I'd be back.

I was sitting down, holding my four-pound preemie girl when the e-mail arrived: "We are unable to grant your request." No explanation. My heart fell. You could say the problems of this workplace discrimination fell into my lap. I dreaded telling my wife, who was upstairs resting, lightheaded from the blood pressure medication. The last thing she needed was this stress.

I appealed to the CEO of Time Warner. He wrote me back saying he'd "look into this." Two days later, when I had heard nothing, I checked in again—this time, copying my attorneys, Lee Parks and Andrew Coffman. (It didn't hurt that they're well known for successfully representing clients in discrimination cases.) I didn't threaten legal action, just asked for prompt attention to the matter, because my family needed me.

Instead, Time Warner informed us that I would not hear from the CEO and that the decision had not changed. So we discussed options. I could stand up and fight by filing a claim for gender discrimination with the Equal Employment Opportunity Commission. It's illegal for a company to retaliate against an employee for filing an EEOC complaint. Still, it happens.

I didn't hesitate. Andrew prepared the filing, charging Time Warner with gender discrimination in the workplace, which is prohibited under Title VII of the Civil Rights Act of 1964. Once Time Warner was informed that we were filing, I waited a day before speaking out publicly, in hopes that Time Warner might reconsider. It didn't. So I released a statement on Tumblr. Here's part of it:

> I have tried repeatedly to get Time Warner to see the light of day on this, but the company refuses. I'm not giving up without a fight. My only remaining hope is that after I post this, other people who also believe in fairness and equality will speak up and encourage Time Warner to do the right thing. A legal battle may drag on forever; my daughter and family need me now. So, in consultation with my attorneys, I'm exercising my First Amendment rights and speaking out.[34]

Lee included this statement in my post:

When you're dealing with paternity leave policies, the current
thinking is that there needs to be equity between what you give a
father and a mother. There can be some disparity, but the disparity here is too great. Giving a mother ten weeks and a father
two weeks is gender-based and violates Title VII. The fact that
adoptive fathers or those who have children through surrogacy get
more time doesn't help the policy—it further erodes the legality
of it. It's evidence that substantiates the irrationality of the policy.[35]

What happened next blew me away. It felt like I had suddenly
thrown open the floodgates of love. After the statement went up
online, hundreds of supportive messages started pouring in. "As a
new dad and fellow TV journalist, I stand in total solidarity with
@joshlevs," well-known broadcaster David Shuster wrote. Friends
and colleagues called, and some even posted their support publicly on
Facebook, unafraid that bosses might see it. A CNN anchor texted
me a thumbs-up.

News agencies called. The *New York Times* put a write-up on the
front page of the business section, under the headline "Standing Up
for the Rights of New Fathers."[36] A big photo showed me holding
my daughter. But I prefer a funny little cartoon image they made of
a man, apparently me, standing outside a door, in a suit, holding his
baby. A suited hand reaches out from inside the doorway, pointing
for him to go away. The article quoted Joan Williams, of the Center
for WorkLife Law, as saying, "The new work-life pioneers are young
egalitarian men exactly like this guy."

NBC's *Today* talked up my case. Cohosts Willie Geist and Al
Roker expressed their support for a dad in my position getting as
many weeks as the parents in the other scenarios I described. "I'm
glad they give the time, but you should even it out somehow," Al said.
Willie agreed. (Natalie Morales, the third host, rightfully emphasized
that better parental leave laws are needed in general.)[37]

ABC.com, *The Huffington Post,* the *Pittsburgh Post-Gazette,* and numerous other media jumped on the story. *Law360,* a daily news site for the legal industry, said lawyers viewed the EEOC charge as "a shot across the bow for employers whose maternity and paternity leave policies may be out of date and an indication that reviewing those policies may be a smart move."[38]

The support I received from men's organizations showed me that the modern dads are the world's greatest fraternity. The army of dad bloggers, whom I had covered as a journalist, were suddenly covering me and made it clear they had my back. The National Fatherhood Initiative (NFI) issued a lengthy statement saying I was "leading the charge."

But it was the effusive support from women that laid the foundation for this book by showing me what a critical women's rights issue this is. Groups like the Lean In organization spread the word quickly. "I have been waiting for somebody to do this publicly," Joan Williams told me.

"More men need to be like you," said Allison Karl O'Kelly, founder of the employment firm Mom Corps. She wants more men to say they need to be at home for the initial weeks of their children's lives. "This is a shared thing on the home front. Companies will see that and not dismiss women as much. It'll just start making sense for families."

It's a catch-22 writing about this, because it seems boastful, which is not at all how I see it. By taking on a sexist policy, I was only doing what a handful of men and many women have done. It shouldn't be rare for a male employee to take a public stance against this kind of discrimination. It's similar to when I started covering fatherhood: something that shouldn't have been revolutionary was.

Time Warner heard the national outcry. It gave the media only a generic statement saying the company had "some of the most progressive and inclusive benefits available. The company's parental leave policy is fair, nondiscriminatory, flexible and available to all employees." ("Obviously it isn't," a colleague said to me.)

Time Warner did not relent, so I went back to work. My colleagues were amazing. They were openly, effusively supportive. "I'm sorry to see you here," one said with a big smile. At first, many stopped by my desk to whisper supportive words. But when some began yelling support across the newsroom—"Good on you, Levs!"—others followed suit. I was hugged and kissed walking through hallways. My back was slapped so much that it got a little sore. A bunch of colleagues started cracking jokes about a ridiculous report I had recently been assigned involving testicles. They decided mine must be "made of titanium." One guy called out to me as I walked into the bathroom, "You're going to change the world, man! You're going down in history!"

No, I won't. Someday it will seem strange that there ever was such a policy to fight. The takeaway here is that if you speak up for something that matters and stand up to authority in a smart way, advised by good attorneys, there will be people who support you. You won't feel alone.

This isn't to say I had no critics, or "haters." There have been a few, most of them anonymous trolls online, whom I always ignore anyway. There are also some people who reject modern manliness in general. Later I'll introduce you to some remaining Neanderthals who equate manhood with ignoring their families and joining spitting contests. (They, and my response to them, made news in 2014, creating what turned out to be a turning point for the country.)

Some people also said my efforts wouldn't achieve anything. Cynics said I shouldn't have stuck my neck out, because corporate America wouldn't budge. But they were proven wrong.

First, shortly after my EEOC filing, Time Warner added a third paid week that applied to dads who have kids the traditional way. It didn't end the discrimination, but at least it was something. Although Time Warner did not publicly link the decision to my action, I had been at the company for years, and the leave was always only two weeks.

Also, dads around the country began taking action. A discrimination hotline run by the Center for WorkLife Law started "getting lots of calls from men in Josh Levs's situation," Joan Williams told *Salon*.[39]

Then came the big change. In October 2014, the same week my daughter turned one, Time Warner's benefits for 2015 were posted online. I knew what to check right away and was thrilled to see the company had changed the policy. "YES!" I posted on social media, along with the hashtag "#ItsAStart."

The change wasn't everything it should have been, but it was great news for the overwhelming majority of both men and women at Time Warner. Now dads like me would get six paid weeks—a giant leap forward. And moms would get even more time after giving birth. Later on I'll explain the complexities of how this works, but the short version is that women would get at least twelve paid weeks after giving birth, with an additional two weeks if a C-section was involved. Since doctors work with women to determine the portion of the leave that's for physical recovery, it could be even more.

Unfortunately, the restructuring of the leave sliced what adoptive parents get down to six weeks. If both parents of an adopted child work for Time Warner, they'll still come out ahead. Now they each get six weeks instead of splitting ten weeks. But if one parent works for Time Warner and the other doesn't, the family loses out. That parent only gets six weeks instead of ten. In a statement celebrating the good parts of the change, I called this part—the decrease for these adoptive and surrogate parents—bad and counterproductive. It should have remained ten weeks for all. As you'll see, many companies have proven that more substantial leave is great for business. But as I wrote in the statement, "In the battle for gender equality, which unites moms and dads, we should stop and celebrate achievements as they come along. Today, we've had one."

A national celebration erupted. Everyone who had spoken out in support of my effort and against the discrimination understood that this was our collective success. "A huge victory for fatherhood and parenting, and hopefully the watershed moment we believe it will be," John Pacini wrote on Twitter. Other messages said the change "made history" and the "crusade will make a tremendous impact." Some fellow Time Warner employees called it a "huge step forward." The company was showing a newfound understanding that, these days, moms and dads are all in this together.

Still, some people worry about me. They fear I'll never get hired anywhere again, that I'll be blacklisted. There's pressure that comes with being the guy whose case is so closely watched. It is risky. My family depends on my income. I'm sure some powerful people in corporate America now see me as a thorn they would not want in their side, which could hurt my chances of getting certain work in the future. If I do pay a professional price, others will get the terrible message not to stand up when it's their turn. And the anonymous trolls I mentioned will have their schadenfreude.

But I have more faith in corporate America than that. I believe many executives are good people who want to do what's right. If we stand up for what we deserve, good things will follow.

We have a long way to go, but together we'll get there. Americans are demanding it, across political lines. There's nothing partisan about wanting to make sure parents get time with their babies while still putting food on the table. A good friend of mine—a mom, proud Tea Party participant, and staunch anti-Obama Libertarian—wants this. So does another good friend, a dad of two and staunch Democrat who voted for Obama twice. Although it may seem impossible these days for our country to be unified on any major policies, surveys show the vast majority of Americans support better, smarter laws and policies and an end to the stigmas.

But in the meantime, these rigid structures are taking a toll on us. They're not just keeping us away from our children. By operating within work structures that haven't stretched out with family life, we're suffering unnecessarily. We're losing sleep, wasting incredible amounts of time in traffic, experiencing a sometimes dangerous level of stress, and missing out on a chance to stop and enjoy each day. Women have done a great job of speaking out about this. It's time for men to join in—in a big way.

"The 'ideal' man today is not only a good employee working long hours to be a successful breadwinner, but is also an involved and nurturing husband/partner, father, and son," the Families and Work Institute wrote in an extensive report about modern expectations of fathers titled "The New Male Mystique."[40] "To truly improve men's lives at work and at home, change needs to occur at all levels—from individual attitudes about work and family to effective workplace design and cultural change that dispels the mystiques for both men and women," said Ken Matos, an author of the report.

He's right. To fix this, we need to change the structures, but also "individual attitudes"—and that includes our own. Some of the changes we can make are under our control. In this book we'll explore steps we can take together to improve life for ourselves and our families.

You'll see new research that reveals how our all-encompassing, frenetic lives are damaging us in mind, body, spirit—and libido. For the first time, you'll learn the truth about how much sex parents are, or aren't, having and how today's more egalitarian parenthood is affecting that. You'll learn why a prominent *New York Times Magazine* cover story was wrong, as were numerous other reports on this.

This book is packed with practical steps and action items we can follow to build better lives and a family-friendly nation. You'll hear from experts across a wide range of fields whose successes have proven what can be done—at work, in the public space, and at home. We can do this. We deserve to.

But first things first. The way to fix all this is to start from day one—from that moment the baby arrives and dads like Doug French are there to help welcome a new life into the world. It's time for a national leave policy that works for all of us. Since the overwhelming majority wants one, why don't we have it? Here are the forces holding us back, how they work, and how we can join together to change them.

PART I

The Parental Leave Battle

Paternity Leave

A Men's and Women's Right

Jay and Kristi Ramsay were excited about the arrival of their second child when they suddenly had a big scare. Thirty-seven weeks into Kristi's pregnancy, the baby stopped moving. The placenta wasn't working. Jay was at work when he got the call. "I frantically jumped out of my seat. I was in panic mode, in tears." He told his office he had a family emergency and ran to his car.

That night, doctors induced. The baby girl was born—fortunately, alive and well. Jay swung back by work the next day, but his boss told him he should go be with his family. So he stayed out for the rest of the week and returned Monday morning. Apparently the three days he took off were too much. When he returned, he was called into a private meeting. "My boss told me I 'should have known better' and 'should have planned better,'" he says. "'Your taking this many days off work? We have so much to do here.'"

Jay was lucky. Just that morning he had learned a new job offer was coming from another company. So in the heat of the moment, he did what virtually all parents would want to do, but can't. "I just leaned forward to her and said, 'I fucking quit right now.' And then I jumped up, took my laptop out of my bag and slammed it down on the desk, as well as my cell phone, and said, 'What else do you need from me, so I can get the hell out of here?' "

"I think it's indicative of society in general," Jay says, speaking at his home in Decatur, Georgia. Some people, he says, think, "Why is the man worrying about the birth of his kids? That's not his concern; that's the woman's job to deal with that. Just keep your head down and work."

Many people are shocked when they find out that the boss in this case was a pregnant woman. But equal rights activists aren't surprised. Gender discrimination is "policed by men, but also, significantly, by women," says Joan Williams.

Our laws aren't helping matters. We don't even provide women with the basics, let alone men. Four in ten workers can lose their jobs for taking time off after having a baby. The Family and Medical Leave Act (FMLA) requires that larger employers allow caregivers— whether female or male—twelve weeks off after a birth. About 40 percent of workers are not covered by FMLA.[1] Worse, some workers entitled to FMLA aren't given it. One in five employers admits not fully complying with FMLA.[2] Who knows how many more just don't admit it.

For workers who do get FMLA, the law doesn't call for any pay. And there's no federal system to provide money during that time. Most families can't afford to halt one income, especially the dominant one, which is most often the father's. A study found so few dads actually take FMLA that "they're almost undetectable." Among that "minuscule" share of dads, most get some pay.[3]

Just over half of U.S. employers offer some paid maternity leave, usually financed through short-term disability.[4] Only about 14 percent offer any paid paternity leave.[5] That includes places that pay for as little as one or two days. And it's getting worse. Employers are cutting back on paid leave.[6]

College professor Josh Azriel is among the millions of men who got no paid leave. He used vacation time. Josh and his wife, Michelle, adopted a child after what he calls a "hellacious two years" of trying to conceive. He would have loved eight or ten paid weeks to help take care of Mia and reduce some of the stress on his wife, he says. "We would have balanced each other out."

Just like most dads of newborns, Josh was soon back at work and running on empty. "A newborn is supposed to be fed every four hours. So I did the 8:00 P.M. feeding and the midnight feeding. I would come home and do a lot of the cooking, the cleaning, and Michelle held Mia for her first year. She rarely put her down. I took on a lot of the tasks of running the home. You get into a routine. It's the feeding, the changing of the diapers, responding to every cry. And you have to take care of yourself, pay the bills, clean the house. Stuff is just falling, left and right."

It's the zombie effect, and you've probably seen it in your office or at the grocery store—the overtired dad with the disheveled shirt and stained tie, somehow managing to get his tasks done. He's the guy with the two diet cokes in the briefcase or gym bag he's carrying around, along with a stash of clean diapers, wipes, and a pacifier, just in case.

The days when most couples had grandparents nearby helping are no more. Young couples move away more often, and older Americans are putting off retirement longer, either because they want to or have to financially.

Dads want to do the caregiving. We love holding our babies, changing them, doing feedings, taking them for walks. It's one of the best feelings on earth. But with no time off from work and loads of responsibilities clogging off-work hours, many men aren't given enough time to.

On the flip side, when dads do get paid paternity leave, the benefits are far-reaching. Those who take it are more deeply involved in their children's lives for years to come. And kids with more involved dads are more likely to excel in all the big ways—in relationships, confidence, academics, the works.

"Those investments we make in infants and young children are some of the most important a society can make," says Heather Boushey, executive director of the Washington Center for Equitable Growth. "Letting parents stay home saves on child-care costs and means kids are healthier. And if dads get engaged, they stay engaged for a lifetime."

Numerous studies show that the best way to engage fathers is through paternity leave. "By drawing fathers into the daily realities of child care, free of workplace constraints, extended time off provides the space necessary for fathers to develop the parenting skills and sense of responsibility that then allows them to be active coparents rather than helpers to their female partners," a study found. That more equitable division of labor often lasts throughout the child's life. Getting started on the right foot requires letting dads be home for more than three weeks, because then "the initial stress and chaos of the immediate post-birth period begins to subside, and patterns and routines develop."[7]

To see this in action, look at Lance and Jessica Somerfeld, of New York. They managed to stay home together for three *months*. "We navigated that landscape, and I think it's one reason why we're more successful as a couple now," Lance says. "The two of us really had no experience with anything in the parenting world. You know, we were those people on an airplane who would be like, 'There's a kid kicking my seat. When's the brat going to cut that out? I'm going on vacation now!' Then all of a sudden the roles are reversed, and it's my kid doing that to someone else.

"The two of us were going up that creek without a paddle. So we were able to really communicate with each other and develop a style that we were comfortable with. We were playing to our strengths and realizing the areas that we weren't so good at, so the other one could pick up the slack."

Lance had worked on Wall Street, rising up the ranks. When he got married, he wanted a better quality of life. "I lost that fire to be a

CEO of a major corporation. I had a very understanding and loving partner, and she was extremely supportive of my taking a leap of faith and trying teaching." He gave up a six-figure salary to teach sixth grade at a public school. When Jessica got pregnant, they both wanted one parent to stay home, and she was among the 23 percent of moms outearning their husbands.[8] So Lance stayed home.

"I was scared shitless, but I was willing to take the leap," he says. Meanwhile, Jessica's work gave her three months of maternity leave, two of which were paid. "We were able for two months to tune out everything else and focus on being good parents and keeping things alive between us as a couple. I learned that I had to be just as good a husband as I was a parent."

Most couples won't be able to stay home at the same time. But men should have the option of staying home for caregiving the same length of time women have. It's best for everyone. "In the long run, the true beneficiaries of paternity leave are women, and the companies and nations that benefit when women advance," Liza Mundy, of the organization New America, wrote in the *Atlantic*. It's "a brilliant and ambitious form of social engineering: a behavior-modification tool that has been shown to boost male participation in the household, enhance female participation in the labor force, and promote gender equity in both domains. The genius of paternity leave is that it shapes domestic and parenting habits as they are forming."[9]

When men can take paternity leave, women have the option of continuing to advance their careers without handing off the kids to others just a few weeks after birth. Most working women who stop their careers after a birth say a central reason is that their husbands had to keep working.[10] And when men get a chance to be caregivers in those early weeks of a baby's life, some decide to give up their jobs, work fewer hours, or work from home—all things that give women more freedom to succeed in the workforce. Sheryl Sandberg calls paid paternity leave necessary to help make men "equal partners and equal parents."

It boils down to simple, basic lack of equality. If policies keep push-ing women to stay home and pushing men to rush back to work, how will women keep working up the ranks? Imagine a husband and wife who work for the same company, and she outranks him. If she gets paid leave and he doesn't, the company is giving her an incen-tive to stay home and him an incentive to stay at work. The chances are that a man will fill in for her while she's out, since in general in America far more men are in higher positions. She loses that time to advance her career; the dad loses the chance to be caregiver in those critical initial weeks; and the child loses out on having two parents equally well equipped and experienced to handle all the caregiving tasks. The business also loses out, because it doesn't get to keep the best talent regardless of gender.

This may all sound well and good, but a big question hovers over it. How would we pay parents for weeks spent not working outside the home without breaking businesses or introducing an exorbitant new tax? Easy. First step: learn the surprising ways billions of dollars are already flowing.

Follow the Money

Our tax system is a joke. If you weren't already familiar with it and I told you about it, you'd be convinced I was making it up. I'd basically have to say, "On this long form with tiny print, subtract line 45e from line 36b and multiply by the number of people in your household, unless you're a redhead in California, in which case you should divide line 46c by the square root of the circumference of the nearest round object on your desk." We're this close to needing a protractor and Ouija board to do taxes in this country.

I say this having covered these issues for years and explained tax implications of the unbelievably complex Affordable Care Act live on TV over and over. But once in a while, something that actually makes simple sense makes it through Congress. And that could happen with paid parental leave for both moms and dads.

Support for it rises far above the partisan bickering that plagues Washington. One poll found 83 percent of adults, including 87 percent of women, support paid leave.[1] Another found 89 percent of dads consider it important.[2] (That figure was a bit inflated, because many of the dads polled were lucky enough to actually have the benefit.) There's a "bipartisan voter mandate for family-friendly workplace policies," the National Partnership for Women and Families says.[3]

The few people opposed to the idea just might change their minds when they learn the facts. Having spoken with people across the political spectrum, I found that those wary of giving parents paid leave assume it would hurt businesses or require some exorbitant tax. But in fact it can be done in a way that helps businesses profit and saves Americans money.

To understand how all this works, we have to start with something big businesses don't like to talk about. What many people refer to as "maternity leave" isn't what you think it is. At some companies, birth moms actually are not given any paid time at all for the purpose of bonding with their children—but dads are.

Here's why. These employers are actually using their disability insurance to pay birth moms during the disability caused by pregnancy and birth. Technically it's like paying a man who broke his legs and can't work. Companies have different plans that determine how much pay their employees get during any disability.

"About 40 percent of employers are covered by disability insurance. It's kind of no skin off their nose" to cover women after a birth, says Heather Boushey, of the Washington Center for Equitable Growth. "Bigger employers already have to give you unpaid time off through FMLA, and your pay is covered by the insurance. They're not doing anything extra, just what they have to do."

And even on this front, things are getting worse. "Employers have become significantly less likely to provide full pay during leave for maternity-related disability," the Families and Work Institute found. Only 9 percent of companies provide full pay, down from 16 percent in 2008.[4]

Until its big policy change, Time Warner was one of these companies having its cake and eating it too. It was praised by some for offering ten weeks of "maternity leave" after a birth, but in reality it was only paying biological moms disability leave. This meant that if a woman was physically capable of coming back to work after only six weeks, technically she had to.

Time Warner had also decided to make ten paid weeks available for "primary caregivers" in nontraditional situations, such as adoption and surrogacy, as I described earlier. This money comes out of corporate coffers.

But a dad who became a parent in the traditional way couldn't get the same ten paid weeks, even to be "primary caregiver." I argued it's time for these distinctions to go away. If people other than birth moms are going to get ten paid weeks for caregiving, the fair way to do it is to make that available to all employees who find themselves in that situation. It isn't an employer's business how the baby came into the world. Fairness would mean tossing all these categories away.

Some experts in this field also oppose policies that apply specifically to "primary" caregivers. "I regularly counsel employers not to set up their leave this way," says Cynthia Calvert, president of Workforce 21C, which helps companies update their policies. "It reinforces the idea that there is one main parent. It also has the effect of excluding men and is difficult for employers to administer."

Attorney Keith Cunningham-Parmeter argues that "by forcing men to prove they are primary caregivers in order to 'earn' paternity leave, (a company) subverts the man's already difficult struggle to obtain some semblance of work-family balance. It's hard enough for a man to challenge workplace norms by asking for such leave at all," he wrote. Telling men that they have to go a step farther and state they are the primary caregiver can be even more intimidating. A man who "musters the courage" to ask, Keith says, "will have to overcome a policy that is predicated on the assumption that parental leave is woman's work."[5]

Time Warner's new policy avoids this conundrum. It provides six paid weeks to any parent. For women who give birth, those six paid weeks are in addition to the paid disability time. Generally, disability leave is six paid weeks after a traditional birth and eight paid weeks after a C-section, but it's up to a doctor to work that out with the mom—so if she needs more time under disability, she gets it.

If we as a nation had the right programs in place, some similar benefits would be available to a lot more workers. The solution is simple and already working out beautifully on the state level.

California pays workers, both men and women, for up to six weeks off to take care of family members. It's funded by a small payroll tax paid by employees. The tax is around 1%, so for every $1,000 you earn, you pay about $10 into the fund. When you need it, you can get up to 55 percent of your pay up to a maximum each week. (The maximum is over $1,000 a week.) The fund operates as part of the state's disability insurance system.[6]

New Jersey and Rhode Island have similar systems. Washington passed a law in 2007 that calls for offering some pay, but the state hasn't found a program to fund it through.[7] Hawaii and New York have programs to pay moms after a birth.[8]

Over the years, there have been efforts to create a national program like this. President Clinton tried to implement one, but it didn't have time to go into effect before President Bush canceled it. Now President Obama is calling for paid leave on a national level. "A few states have acted on their own to give workers paid family leave, but this should be available to everyone, because all Americans should be able to afford to care for a family member in need," he said.[9] In 2015, the president announced some new initiatives. But, as this book goes to press, the president has not called for a law establishing paid family leave for everyone.

He did take a big step forward for federal workers. Obama signed a Presidential Memorandum allowing them to take six paid weeks of sick leave after having a child—but it comes out of their pile of accrued sick leave or the leave they will accrue in the future. The president also called on Congress to pass a law establishing "six weeks of paid administrative leave for the birth, adoption, or foster placement of a child." That would allow federal workers the time without having to use their sick leave. A bill has been introduced, but as this book goes to press, it's unclear whether a law will pass.

As for those of us who don't work for the federal government, here's what the president proposed: funding to help some states create their own programs. His budget request included $2.2 billion to reimburse up to five states for three years "for the administrative costs and roughly half of the cost of benefits associated with implementing" a paid family leave program. The Department of Labor is also kicking in $1 million in competitive grants for "six to ten states or municipalities to conduct paid leave feasibility studies."[10]

There is, no doubt, a political strategy to this. "Democrats are seizing on the fight for mandatory paid leave in the United States as their next big pocketbook issue," *The Hill* reported. It quoted AFL-CIO secretary treasurer Elizabeth Shuler as saying "2016 will be the year people start making it a pillar of their economic platform."[11]

Congress has talked up this issue before, to no avail. The Majority Staff of the congressional Joint Economic Committee tried to address the issue of "a clear gender gap" in access to paid family leave:

> The equality in the availability of sick days and unpaid family leave does not make up for the lack of fathers' access to paid family leave. Fathers (and mothers) may need their sick days to help care for a sick child or their own illness. Further, in two-thirds of two-earner couples, the husband earns more than the wife and therefore, for many families, it is harder for the father to take unpaid time off work, because it costs the family more in terms of lost wages. Moving toward greater equality in access to paid family leave would enable more fathers to bond with and care for their new children, while continuing to recognize that childbirth requires recovery for the mother. . . .
>
> While mothers need more time to recover physically from the rigors of childbirth and to breastfeed, fathers are also needed at home to help care for the new child. New paid family-leave policies should follow the FMLA and allow both mothers and

fathers similar lengths of time to care for and bond with a new child. . . . Paid parental leave is part of a broader set of new workplace policies that Americans need to meet the competing demands of work and family.[12]

For all the talk, we've gotten nowhere. Now several groups actively pursuing this issue have aligned with lawmakers to try to change that. Heather Boushey is a driving force behind the FAMILY Act. "For twelve weeks, you will get paid. It will be financed by a small tax on everyone who works, and everyone will be eligible as long as they have employment history," she says.

You'd get two-thirds of your wages, up to a maximum of $4,000 a month. To fund it, with each paycheck you'd pay two cents for every ten dollars you make. Employers would pay the same. The cost "is not that much money," Boushey says. "This is not going to lead to some massive increase in prices or costs. This is a very small bite for what in reality is a huge benefit for families and employers."

It applies to any worker who needs to take care of a family member. That should help mitigate a complaint that often pops up, albeit by just a relatively small number of people. They say, according to Keith Cunningham-Parmeter, "Why should society fund individuals' personal procreative decisions?" Some of the people complaining, he says, call parents "breeders." Some of the anonymous riffraff who posted responses online to the news of my EEOC charge said similar things. They clearly didn't know the facts of my case and argued that if I was concerned about money, I shouldn't have had another child.

Given that local taxes pay for public schools and that kids can be covered by Medicaid, it seems we're all paying for at least some of each other's "procreative decisions." Ta-Nehisi Coates, a stay-at-home dad who writes for the *Atlantic*, characterizes such complaints this way: "How dare you try to propagate the species? I can't believe that you're making more Americans!"[13]

But even these people will have a tougher time arguing against leave for anyone to care for a family member. "The truth of our time is we're all going to be working and we're all going to be taking care of someone," Liza Mundy says.

Still, some people believe a law is not the answer. "A top-down solution isn't going to work," says Nita Ghei, who wrote a column for the Cato Institute opposing paid family leave. "You end up with unintended consequences."

One is the cost of implementing a program. That's something I want to know as well. An official document proposing the FAMILY Act states that there would be a cost to implement it, to be paid back within ten years.[14] I requested the figure, and was told it's not immediately available. But the Center for American Progress says the act would "create an independent trust fund within the Social Security Administration to collect fees and provide benefits. In other words, the system is already set up and can be expanded efficiently."[15]

Ghei also worries that a federal law "stops people from experimenting, from saying, 'Let's see if there are other innovative ways of retaining valuable employees.'" She prefers "lowering tax burdens and regulatory burdens generally," which would help people save money, so that they'd have a choice about one parent staying home longer. For example, Ghei wants a more generous Earned Income Tax Credit, which allows a tax break for people who make "low to moderate income." But Ghei also originally opposed FMLA—and now, seeing how it's played out, she says, "My gut feeling is, this is one of the ones that's worth keeping."

Jim Daly, president of the conservative group Focus on the Family, goes a step farther. "In hindsight, I'm a little embarrassed that I and others fought that idea of FMLA," he says. "You know what? If we're honest, when we look back on it, it was good for families. We should have been at the forefront saying, 'Maybe this is good.'

"There's got to be a point of diminishing return," Jim went on to say. "You have to work, you can't take every day off. But I think right now in our culture policies that contribute to the stability of the family need to be pursued. And this is something, if we could put the party rhetoric down for a minute, I think giving a nod to President Clinton for FMLA, what the Democrats did there, I think that's a good thing in hindsight. We should not have been so apprehensive."

From years as a journalist covering politics and being far outside the Beltway, I've seen that there's much more common ground than our political system lets on. The vast majority of Americans are good people who want life to be better for American families and really agree on a lot. It's the Washington campaign-money political echo that makes us feel so torn apart. Jim Daly agrees. "I think people have to open their eyes to that," he says.

Former president Clinton says, "I have had more people mention the family leave law to me, both while I was in the White House and in the twelve years since I've been gone, than any other single piece of legislation I signed. . . . People desperately want to have successful families, to be good parents, to have a job and succeed at it. If you take one away to get the other, the country pays a grievous price and every life is diminished."[16]

Some Democratic lawmakers are pushing for the FAMILY Act, including Senator Kirsten Gillibrand of New York. "The Family and Medical Leave Act we have today first passed with strong, bipartisan support—because Democrats and Republicans in Congress agreed on this very basic principle of job security," she wrote in the *New York Daily News*. "Nothing should stop us from updating this law to meet the demands of our families and the new economy—by creating paid family and medical leave for every worker in America."[17]

The growing calls for paid family leave should help draw support from some Republican leaders and conservative groups that have traditionally eschewed these ideas. In fact, these groups already seem to be quieting down or even halting their opposition. It's very rare these days to find an organization that wants to argue publicly against paid family leave. That could signal a sea change in American politics.

In 2009, *Newsweek*'s staff published an editorial entitled "The

Argument Against Paid Family Leave."[18] I tried repeatedly to get anyone involved at *Newsweek,* then or now, to talk to me about it for this book, but no one got back in touch. At this point, it's not even clear whether *Newsweek* stands by it.

The editorial said lowering taxes would help women more and that a federal law aimed at keeping people in the workforce full-time might not be what's best for families. It also said that sometimes laws aimed at helping people backfire, like the 1990 Americans with Disabilities Act. "Employers, faced with the cost of accommodation and the threat of litigation, chose the rational option: they cut back on hiring the disabled. When the cost of hiring a worker rises, demand for that worker falls. Mandated paid family leave will have the same effect on women for precisely the same reasons."[19]

After President Obama announced the new steps he was calling for in 2015, a small conservative women's group called the Independent Women's Forum spoke out against government mandates for paid leave.

"There are trade-offs between benefits and take-home pay and we have to allow workers and employers to find situations that benefit both parties," the group's managing director Carrie Lukas said in a statement.

When we spoke, Carrie told me she's concerned that since women are more likely to use paid leave, employers will be less likely to put them in leadership positions—because it would mean holding those leadership positions open while these women take time off. "There's no way people can lobotomize themselves to not know that" when making hiring decisions, she said.

Carrie pointed out that the OECD has found women are still sorely lacking in senior positions in European countries that have mandated leave policies.[20] That's true, but there are numerous reasons for it. "The barriers that remain derive from a combination of stereotypical attitudes and perceptions, which continue to compartmentalize people and leadership qualities by gender," the European

Commission said in a report. And those attitudes affect both home and work.

This will improve as more men start taking leave. Making "leave arrangements equally available to men and women should help to diminish the view that early-stage child care is solely a female responsibility," the commission said.[21]

Carrie wants the government to keep out of this issue. She praised companies that offer flexibility and those that hold jobs for women while they take extended unpaid leave, offering piece work and training to help ease them back into the job market after. But while Carrie's organization spoke out, the big groups that previously led the charge against paid family leave programs didn't.

In the past, the U.S. Chamber of Commerce has fought against efforts to establish paid family-leave programs. In 2007 Randy Johnson, then vice president of the chamber, said the business community would wage "all-out war" against such a program for two reasons: "someone's got to pay for it," and it would give employees incentive to use the benefit even if it's inappropriate.[22] The chamber filed a lawsuit against the federal government opposing the Clinton-era effort to establish paid leave. In a court filing, the chamber argued that the government can't use unemployment funds to pay employed workers for time off, which the program called for. It also said the government had failed to consider the impact on small businesses.[23] Since the Clinton effort never came to fruition, the suit was dropped.

I contacted the chamber to talk about this issue, but it offered no public position or statement and no comment. It's possible the chamber's position is softening. *Forbes* notes that the organization has been praised for implementing its own paid-leave program providing up to ten days so employees can care for family members.[24] It also implemented subsidized backup care for employees' families.

Another group that has vociferously opposed paid leave is the Society for Human Resource Management. "At a time when there are soaring deficits and many business are still struggling, paid leave becomes yet another entitlement program," Lisa Horn, senior government relations adviser, told the *Washington Post* in 2013. "That's a difficult pill for the business community to swallow."[25] But now, given a chance to speak out in this book, the group didn't comment. Neither did the National Federation of Independent Business, which says on its website that it opposes paid family laws at both the state and federal level, because "the added benefits can be hard for small businesses to afford."

I can't know why they didn't comment, but I can tell you this. Ever since new studies came out showing that paid leave laws are actually helping businesses, these groups have been mysteriously reticent. That makes sense. If your organization exists to help businesses be the best job providers they can be, why would you fight something that, according to the latest information available, would actually help?

"That's the nice thing about facts," says Heather Boushey. She's right. The cat is now out of the bag, America. Paid family leave—as you're about to see—is a proven boon for business.

Paid Family Leave

Good for Business

Shaun Leighton has the kind of job many people dream of. He's COO of a national law firm. It's work Shaun believes in and profits from. But there's another reason this father of two joined the company—it offers dads six paid weeks off after the birth of a child.

"For me it signaled a firm that was willing to work with parents and be flexible and one that valued family life as much as it valued work life. I didn't want to be in a situation where I was getting a two-week vacation and didn't get to spend time with my kids. I wanted to be part of their lives early on, to be there and take the time from when they're born, and to support my wife as well when she went through that."

Brian Stephens also loved his job, as a communications director for a professional association. But after his son was born, he quit. The company offered dads four paid weeks off, but he wanted to be home for more of his son's earliest days. So he stayed home while his partner worked. His company lost a valuable employee and had to go through the expense of recruiting, hiring, and training someone new. That new employee still wouldn't be as skilled and up-to-speed on the firm's inner workings as Brian.

Companies are starting to see this reality: paid paternity leave helps attract and retain employees. Dads who get none, or like Brian don't get as much as they're looking for, sometimes quit and find jobs elsewhere. "I have had both women and men who've said, 'I came here because of your policies, and because of what it says about rewarding and wanting fatherhood,'" Sheryl Sandberg says of Facebook, which gives both moms and dads seventeen paid weeks.

In the coming years, it will be impossible for the largest employers to lure top talent without offering substantial leave to dads. Among millennial men especially, the ability to stay home with children after a birth is increasingly important. "They're not going to do what their fathers did, which is to not even ask for time off or to back off immediately if they ask and don't get it," says Joan Williams. "So it doesn't make sense for an employer who wants to attract the best and the brightest to say, 'We want all the best and the brightest, as long as they have an extremely traditional view about fathers.' And that's really what corporate America is doing today."

"Some employers feel that if they give men reasonable paternity leave, they're going to have to give everyone leave for everything. You know, it's a floodgate issue," says attorney Cynthia Calvert. "That's really not a good argument, because employers who have provided paid paternity leave have had no trouble drawing the line. Moreover, the workforce has changed. You have to give the workforce what it wants or you're going to lose your good, trained, experienced workers who have relationships with your customers and clients. To attract and retain Gen X, now Gen Y, you have to take care of these lifestyle needs."

Jay Ramsay says if he was offered a job at another company for $10,000 more per year but no paternity leave or flexibility to be with his family, he might turn it down. "For $20,000 I wouldn't care," he says with a smile.

"What about $15,000?" I ask.

"I'd flip a coin!"

Millions of young dads are like Jay. They want successful careers, but family comes first. Businesses that understand this have a big leg up. "There's a war for talent," says Brad Harrington, of the Center for Work and Family. To attract and keep the most highly skilled employees, "companies need to come up with ways to relieve pressures and have people realize a life outside of work." An office "that includes a family-supportive culture, supportive managers, and supportive coworkers leads to better alignment between work and family, and also leads to more satisfied employees who are less likely to leave the company," Harrington's office found in a study.[1]

Don Jackson, a dad in St. Louis, thinks employers and hiring managers should love committed parents of both genders. "Isn't it a true sign of character if you want to stay home with your kid? You get loyalty. You get someone who's willing to do things that are tough."

Morgan Stanley has figured that out. It now provides sixteen paid weeks for primary caregivers. "I've seen the benefits of fair family leave," Tom Nides, managing director and vice president, wrote in a *Huffington Post* column. The company's policy, he said, is "a benefit both to families and to the firm. Demonstrating this type of loyalty and respect for our people reinforces the same in return."[2]

Bank of America offers twelve paid weeks for moms, dads, and adoptive parents. The policy "was included in our comprehensive benefits program in order to meet the diverse needs of our employees to help them manage the needs of their families," says spokeswoman Ferris Morrison. "Many of our employees take advantage of our paternity-leave policy each year. Through our regular efforts to listen to employees and evaluate how our benefits are meeting their needs, we hear that our paternity, maternity, and adoptive leave programs are highly valued by both men and women." Deloitte offers eight paid weeks to whichever parent will be primary caregiver, regardless of gender. Yahoo gives dads eight paid weeks; moms get sixteen. Google gives moms twenty-two paid weeks and dads twelve. Ernst & Young gives dads six—and allows moms as much as thirty-nine weeks of paid leave.

It isn't just big companies. Some small businesses are leading the way as well. At an eighteen-employee Boston nonprofit called Keshet, all employees who have worked for the organization at least two years are given three months of paid leave to care for a new child, no matter how that child came into the employee's life. "In the long term, I believe that in addition to being the right thing to do, our family-leave policy helps us keep and attract top level staff," says executive director Idit Klein.

This argument—that it helps attract and retain excellent employees—could actually be seen as an argument *against* a law requiring paid leave. After all, if there's a business incentive, the "free market" will just make family leave happen, right? Cali Williams Yost, a former banker and business consultant, argues that businesses would do much better with a paid leave law. She wrote an article for *Forbes* called "Three Reasons Why Card-Carrying Capitalists Should Support Paid Family Leave":

> When faced with the choice between family and work, people
> will often choose family even if it means financial hardship.
> When someone quits without paid leave, especially a low wage
> worker, they are often forced to apply for public assistance
> which is paid by taxpayers. Wouldn't it be better to contribute
> to universal paid leave that lasts six weeks versus enrollment in
> public assistance that could go on much longer if the individual
> can't find a new job?
>
> Losing an employee is very expensive. Experts estimate it
> can cost anywhere from 50 percent of the wages of a low skilled
> employee to 200 percent of the salary of a professional staff
> person. Wouldn't it be better to lose someone temporarily for six
> weeks, knowing they will come back, versus having a valuable
> employee quit because of caregiving pressures and replacing
> them? There is no guarantee the next person you hire—male or
> female—won't experience caregiving challenges either.[3]

Yost also argues that a uniform law could help companies organize and prepare for staff to be out for specific amounts of time, helping them plan.

A law could also help small businesses compete for the same workers as big corporations, because the mandated benefit would apply at either place. And it would take the costs out of corporate coffers. "If the state contributed funds to parental leave costs, that would certainly be good for our bottom line and, more importantly, send a key message about investing in family and child development," says Idit Klein.

There are even more arguments in favor of a law. Leaving it up to free-market competition could take a very, very long time, and this problem needs an immediate solution. Also, the free-market solution would leave out many people. "Researchers have found that many workers appear to have limited ability to bargain for these benefits," a study by the Center for American Progress found. "The workers who most need workplace flexibility report having the least access to it. For example, a young worker who is planning to start a family but who finds employment at a business with fewer than fifty employees may have no choice but to take the available job, despite a lack of guaranteed access to paid or unpaid parental leave. Access to job-protected or paid time off, such as paid parental leave, will shape who actually takes time off."[4]

A paid leave law "would make a huge difference, especially for workers with less education who are the least likely to take time away from work to care for a new child," the study found. "Care in the first few months of a child's life is key to ensuring that child starts out on the right track for the rest of his or her life. Parents should not have to choose between a paycheck and caring for a newborn during these crucial months."[5]

Fortunately, talk of how parental leave plays out isn't just hypothetical. We now know how it affects American businesses. "The business community's concerns prior to passage of the PFL (Paid Family Leave) legislation, that it would impose extensive new costs

on employers and involve a particularly serious burden for small businesses, were unfounded," according to the Center for Economic and
Policy Research, which examined the impacts of California's law on
the state's employers. The vast majority said the law had minimal
impact on their operations and that it had either a positive effect or
no noticeable effect on productivity and profits. Virtually all said the
law either improved or didn't affect employee turnover and morale.
Small businesses were even less likely than larger companies to report
any problems.[6]

"Employers raised strong concerns prior to implementation about
abuse of the program. However the vast majority (91 percent) of re-
spondents to the employer survey said 'No' when asked if they were
'aware of any instances in which employees that you are responsible
for abused the state Paid Family Leave program,'" the study found.

What the state's paid leave has done is striking. Women who used
it ended up breastfeeding their children twice as many weeks on average. "Substantially" more men took bonding leave, since they could
afford to. And men took longer leaves. They "used to take only two
weeks off when they had a new child, using sick leave and/or vacation
time. Today, new fathers typically take around five to six weeks of
bonding leave," an HR manager for a large manufacturing firm said.
The manager at corporate headquarters of a food-processing business
said that before the law, it was rare for men to take any significant
time off after a birth. Now both white-collar and blue-collar male
workers are taking the time off.

Meanwhile, researcher Sharon Lerner, of the public-policy group
Demos, explored how a similar program is working in New Jersey.
She writes:

> Despite the diversity of the eighteen businesses I wound up visit-
> ing, which spanned the gamut from shipping to home nursing,
> pharmaceutical, and accounting, most of the owners or human
> resources managers I spoke with said the same thing: that paid

leave hadn't affected how they do business. Not a single company felt it affected turnover or productivity. And while some had feared employees would take advantage of the program—receiving benefits they weren't due, for example—no one knew of any instances of abuse actually happening.

Perhaps surprisingly, since some had predicted the law would be so burdensome it would drive businesses from the state, many employers said they actually liked the program. When I asked how it had affected their work "all in all," none responded negatively. Six saw the law as neutral, while twelve felt it had a positive impact.[7]

The Center for Women and Work at Rutgers University, in New Jersey, found that "providing paid family leave to workers leads to positive economic outcomes for working families, businesses and the public."[8] Women are far more likely to still be in the workforce more than a year later. Paid leave is also linked to "reduced spending by businesses in the form of employee replacement costs, and by governments in the form of public assistance," researcher Linda Houser said. Women who took paid leave are 39 percent less likely to receive public assistance and 40 percent less likely to receive food stamps a year later.

Some fiscal conservatives who have seen these results say they want a law that makes at least some paid leave available. "I'm a Republican," says Allison Karl O'Kelly, of Mom Corps. "I'd like as few laws as possible around this stuff. I'd like companies to make this a benefit so people want to work for these companies, and they get better employees. The free market is kind of who I am. That being said, I recognize that at the lower-income jobs there does need to be some base."

The arguments in favor of paid family leave are overwhelming. But that's in the real world. In Washington, where federal laws are made, reality doesn't always play much of a role. The motto for Capitol Hill is often: "Facts, schmacts." After years of covering tax issues and politics and watching facts get twisted, I see how easily paid family leave can be shot down. It's the reductive messaging that destroys political debate, a sickness that prevents us from moving forward on all sorts of issues.

There's one glaring reason that the current paid family-leave proposals could fall victim to that. Any lawmaker who supports them can technically be accused of "voting to increase taxes." Never mind that the "increase" could be just twenty cents for every hundred dollars you make and that you'd get that money back in kind when you need it to take care of a family member. In any campaign season, which is every other year for Congress, that's an attack most lawmakers just don't want to face.

Given that one in four Americans doesn't even know the earth revolves around the sun, we can't count on some voters to see through the political ads.[9] And my industry, the news media, needs to do a much better job of bringing the national conversation around to facts instead of horse-race analysis. (It isn't our job to relentlessly ask pundits whether certain attacks will work. It's our job to fight for the whole truth.)

So any bill could easily die in committee or in either chamber of Congress. One of the most prominent political figures says so herself. "I don't think, politically, we could get it now," said former Secretary of State Hillary Clinton, who as this book goes to press is widely considered a contender for the presidency. Paid maternity leave should be law "eventually," Clinton said at a CNN town-hall event. But for now the country is doing "what we have done in various parts of our history in the past. States try things out. And then we check to see how it's working, and then we try to take it to the national level."[10]

Keith Cunningham-Parmeter, one of the few male attorneys focused largely on fighting for better policies, also thinks state-level efforts are more promising. "States are much more innovative on this front. It's cheaper to try different models. And I think the political will exists in some states to do this, whereas federally it's nowhere in sight."

But Heather Boushey says there needs to be a federal law. Like Washington state, some other states don't currently have the infrastructure to fund this kind of program. "The smartest, most efficient way to do it is to build it within the Social Security infrastructure," she says.

Proponents of this point out that the United States is an outlier in the world for having no guaranteed paid time off, even for moms. They're right. It's literally just us, Papua New Guinea, Suriname, and a few tiny islands.[11] There were two other small nations on that list, Lesotho and Sierra Leone, but both implemented paid maternity leave in recent years. So of the few people on earth who live in countries without mandatory paid maternity leave, 98 percent are Americans. We're also among just a handful of nations that have not ratified the U.N. Convention on the Elimination of All Forms of Discrimination Against Women (CEDAW), which calls for paid maternity leave.[12] It was established in 1981.

Much of the world also has paid paternity leave, including Russia, western Europe, parts of Africa, and most of South America. Even in Saudi Arabia, where gender laws are so backward that women are fighting for the right to drive, dads are required to get a day of paid paternity leave.[13]

More countries are establishing paid paternity leave. "Recognition of men's right to parenthood as well as of their responsibility to share unpaid care and household work will help to break down traditional social attitudes, resulting in greater equality for both men and women at work and at home," the International Labour Organization says.[14] It calls for "paternity and/or parental leave with incentives to encourage men to take up such leave."[15]

But what works elsewhere isn't much of an argument in the United States, says Brad Harrington. "America has kind of painted a picture that government intrusion is never in the best interest of economic growth. In other countries that have different attitudes about the role of government or social welfare, they would take a different stance."

So if we're going to make paid family leave happen, it will be through an orchestrated effort to rise up and demand it. Congress needs to hear the call from moms and dads like Jeff Bogle, of Exton, Pennsylvania. "What matters is forming bonds and making memories. None of that happens if newborns are in day care," he says. "Politicians say, 'We have to take care of the children, but get back to work.' Better laws would be a wonderful thing. I'd be willing to pay the tax to help people stay home longer with their babies. The trickle-down effect for society would be worth it."

All parents should join this discussion and have their voices heard. Some want a law that goes far beyond anything being discussed in Washington. Adrienne Martin, mom of two girls in Atlanta, would like "a policy in which parents alternated time across a year, and ideally it would be paid." Three months isn't "enough time for parents to bond with babies, to really give them the foundation they need to go off into the world. What three-month-old person is ready to be turned over to strangers to be taken care of while the parents go to work?"

There are also parents who seek more limited laws. Richard Dorment, of *Esquire,* wants mandatory paid maternity leave for biological mothers, but doesn't believe the law should have to cover dads. "I think paternity leave is important, and I think companies should offer it. But I don't think it should be conflated with maternity leave, which has a lot more issues, most of them physical and biological."

When I began doing the research for this book, I didn't have a position on whether there should be a paid family-leave law. But everything I've learned has taught me that the answer is yes. So if the ideas already being proposed can't pass due to political gamesmanship, I propose another idea. One that would turn the political argument on its head. After all, who in Congress wants to vote against *lowering* taxes?

How to Cover Family Leave by Lowering Taxes

A great piece of advice I got as a kid: Turn every disadvantage into an advantage. If the biggest disadvantage for lawmakers supporting paid family leave is that they can be accused of wanting to "raise taxes," what if we flip the script? What if anyone *opposing* paid family leave is voting to raise taxes?

Here's what I'd love to see: a 401(k) type of program for family leave. Workers would be allowed to set aside some portion of their pay tax free, perhaps 5 percent, up to a legal cap. It would go into a fund they could access when they have a qualifying situation not covered by their employer's disability plan (or by a paid leave plan if the employer has one). They would get something similar to what's being proposed in the FAMILY Act—two-thirds of their salary, up to a weekly maximum, until the funds are exhausted. Unused funds could be cashed in eventually, but then taxes would have to be paid on them.

Lawmakers may be wary of the idea, fearing it would decrease tax revenue at a time when the country is in ridiculous debt. But in fact it would increase tax revenue. Numerous studies show that employees are dropping out of the workforce to take care of loved ones.

That means they're not contributing to corporate productivity and not paying income taxes. So the entire economy shrinks. Allowing people to use their own saved, tax-free money for time off while caregiving would make it much more likely that they would return to the workforce.

One flaw in this plan is that younger workers having children would have had fewer years to save up money. But they could at least have saved *something,* which is a big step above the nothing many workers have access to now. And this proposal might have a better shot at actually passing.

It would also help us get back some of what the Affordable Care Act took away. Before that law, many U.S. workers could put away up to $5,000 tax free in a Flexible Spending Account to cover medical expenses.[1] The law chopped that in half to $2,500. So, like many other Americans, I'm now paying taxes on $2,500 of annual income that was previously tax free. A 401(k)-style savings plan for family leave could restore that and more. And knowing that it's tax free would give people incentive to save.

I asked many people of different perspectives to poke holes in this idea, but got support for it. "If you're going to manipulate the tax system, I'd rather you do it that way," said Nita Ghei, who was with the Cato Institute and is now with the Mercatus Center at George Mason University.

"I'm a little embarrassed I never would have thought of that," said dad blogger Jeff Bogle. "I believe in saving for current life experiences rather than just end-of-life experiences."

Still, I know this may be a pie-in-the-sky idea. Consider it an out-of-the-box suggestion to help get discussions going. If the current paid family leave ideas floating in Congress fail, let's come up with new ones. I'm a big believer that in this country, despite Washington gridlock, we the people can push through creative solutions that work.

Ready to fight for sensible policies? Here are ten steps to take:

1. Spread the word. Share the information in this book exposing the truth about paid family leave that covers both men and women.

2. Call and write lawmakers at both the state and federal levels. Tell your representatives and senators that you support these policies and why. Ask them where they stand and demand that they give reasons for their positions.

3. Organize in person. Gather groups of like-minded parents to discuss what can be done in your state. Create petitions. Tell neighbors and friends. The bigger your group, the louder its voice.

4. Organize online. Join groups that are pushing for these policies, and sign up for their newsletters. (You'll find links at this book's website.) Create a website for the local group you created—even something simple like a web page or blog. Post your thoughts and experiences for the world to see on Facebook, Twitter, Pinterest, Google Plus, Tumblr, and anywhere else. (Make those posts public.)

5. Show up at town-hall events and debates. In years of covering local races that are of interest to the nation, I've seen how sparsely attended some are. Most—which take place in the months before local, state, and federal elections—allow questions from the crowd. Be there. Be respectful. Be heard. In asking your question, begin by listing a few facts from this book that demonstrate the value of sensible family leave.

6. Reach out through the media. Let local and national media know about events your group is holding to push for sensible family leave on the state and/or national levels. Offer interviews with group members whose stories best exemplify how today's dads and moms are all-in parenting together—and how badly we need new laws and policies.

7. Coordinate with other groups. Get to know the groups all over the country helping lead the way. (You'll see a list at the website for this book.) Hold a social media day in which you popularize a hashtag, like AllIn.

8. Calculate. How many people in your group have left or turned down jobs, missed critical family events, or suffered in other ways due to the lack of sensible policies? Show both sides—how businesses and employees are losing out. Put these figures on your website and offer them to the media. (For example, "The twenty-eight people in this local organization have turned down a combined forty-seven jobs, and nine members have quit jobs they otherwise liked, all because of the lack of sensible parental leave.")

9. Brainstorm. What unique events would make a splash where you live and get media coverage? A YouTube video? In the next holiday parade, a giant float of a baby in a diaper with a sign on her tummy that says, "Mommy and Daddy Need Family Leave"? Don't be afraid to be creative. Embrace it.

10. Gather in Washington. Gather moms and dads of all backgrounds one weekend day for a rally on the mall in support of paid family leave.

There's an irony to all of this. We need to push for paid family leave even though many dads who are currently allowed some aren't using all of it. We're effectively leaving billions of dollars on the table. That's because of a problem that runs deep in our culture.

The Stigma That Makes Men
Give Up Billions

The way much of corporate America sees it, a guy who gives up wild adventures and late nights of beer chugging to stay home and care for his children is trading in manliness for femininity. That's why terms like "Mr. Mom" persist, despite organized campaigns to end the term. "1983 was Mr. Mom's Year," says Chris Bernholdt, of Devon, Pennsylvania, who runs the blog DadNCharge. "These days," he says, "just call me dad."

Well-meaning people make this mistake, thinking they're praising dads. It's based on a mistaken belief that when left alone in nature, women would care for their young while men would just grunt and walk away. Today's dads recognize that committing to fatherhood is the manliest thing they've ever done.

There may be no better example than Don Jackson. He can't tell you what he used to do for the federal government. It's a secret. "I couldn't continue to do the job and have a kid," he says mysteriously, adding that giving up that line of work "was about making sure I protect my family."

The six-foot-tall, broad-shouldered dad from St. Louis admits that it involved physical strength. That came in handy during his wife's childbirth, when she squeezed his hand so hard that she crushed it, fracturing his right pinky finger. "I didn't realize it until three days later," he says. "It was excruciating pain, but I didn't want to complain."

Don's descriptions of his former life conjure up images of action movies and classic, brooding masculinity. But Don left that life behind. "I jumped off the cliff," he says. "I love being a dad way more than that. It's the job I always wanted."

Don is a cancer survivor. And he's raising one as well, as stepfather to his girlfriend's son who got testicular cancer at eighteen months. The couple also has a young son together. "If you love what you do, you'll never work a day in your life," Don says. "For me, that's what being a parent, a dad, is. I wake up, and it's awesome. I was up for forty-eight straight hours, because my son had stomach flu. He threw up all over. We finally went into the bathroom, and I thought, what other person would I do this for? I used to be the kind of person who wouldn't let anyone eat off my plate or drink from my glass."

Don now works part-time from home for a media group, making a lot less money than he used to. He focuses primarily on raising the two boys. His stepson, now nine, lost one testicle to cancer. And the radiation at such a young age caused some walking trouble, hearing loss, and weak eyesight, "so he wears these Sally Jesse Raphael glasses," Don jokes. Raising these two boys, Don says, is as manly as it gets.

He's right. For fathers, manliness means living up to the responsibilities you have to your family. And those responsibilities are no longer primarily about money. Six in ten Americans now say the most important role of a father is to teach morals and values to his children. Most also say dads should provide emotional support and discipline. Making money is now relatively far down the list. Only four in ten believe it's even among a father's most important responsibilities.[1]

But at work, old stereotypes prevail. "Men who take leave or adopt flexible schedules are seen as bad workers. And that 'bad worker effect' is totally explained by the fact that they're seen as inappro-

priately 'feminine,' " says Joan Williams, of the Center for WorkLife
Law. Her working group carried out four separate studies. All came
back with similar results.

One found that men who take their twelve weeks of federally
mandated unpaid family leave to care for a sick child or an ailing
parent often end up demoted or let go altogether.[2] Another found
that men who take career breaks or reduce hours for family reasons
get sharply reduced earnings when they return to their previous
schedules.[3] A third found that men who work part-time to care for
their newborns "are seen as more feminine and less masculine" and
therefore as "gender deviants."[4]

The fourth study found that "caregiving fathers experience more
harassment and mistreatment than traditional fathers and men without children."[5] And this one involved men in Canada, which is ahead
of the United States on these issues. Both moms and dads have access
to some paid leave; they can stay home for about nine months, and
employers are required to reinstate them at the same salary level
when they come back. Employers even have to raise their pay if the
wages for the work went up while they were out. Yet even Canadian
dads face this stigma.

"Men who do the low-status 'feminine' work of child care and
housework are likely to be seen as failed men. They are also likely to
be seen as having their dedication split between work and home, and
therefore as bad workers," the study said. Colleagues and bosses often
see these men as "wimps" with wives who "wear the pants."[6]

The need to prove masculinity is keeping men at the office for
far too many hours, the studies found. Joan Williams compares it
to a classic, ridiculous, manliness competition. "The way you signal
that you are a go-getter—and 'yours is the biggest'—is by having the
biggest schedule," she says. The obsession with hours rather than productivity is also a major factor holding women back, because mothers
are less likely to work very long hours.

"If you define the ideal worker as someone who starts to work in early adulthood and works full-time, full force for forty straight years, not taking time off for child rearing or anything else, this describes men in traditional families," Williams says. "Since I started to work on these issues in 1988, families have changed, but workplaces haven't. I'm completely astonished."

It's a problem former Supreme Court Chief Justice William Rehnquist has railed against. In a court opinion he wrote:

> Stereotypes about women's domestic roles are reinforced by parallel stereotypes presuming a lack of domestic responsibilities for men. . . . These mutually reinforcing stereotypes created a self-fulfilling cycle of discrimination that forced women to continue to assume the role of primary family caregiver, and fostered employers' stereotypical views about women's commitment to work and their value as employees.[7]

A retired judge in Georgia told me it's something she has noticed throughout her life. "I had options. My brothers did not," says Leah Ward Sears, the first African American woman to serve as a state supreme court chief justice. "To be 'real men,' they had to go to work. I could work or stay home and be a 'real woman.'"

"Men hold men back," she adds. "Men have the power and men have the cards. And the men who are the power brokers have a certain sense of what a man is."

After I announced my legal fight, dads around the country started bringing me their stories. "I was offered two weeks' paternity leave. I took one week, and my boss pretty much threatened that if I didn't come back then, I wouldn't have a job," says Adam Cohen, of New York City. "He was one of those old-school, non-PC guys."

Jeff Porzio worked for one of the world's biggest advertising companies. After the birth of his child, he took off only one week, though he could have taken two. The pressure to not use both paid weeks was "social, indirect," he says. "It felt like a PR benefit, not a real benefit"—just there on paper to make the company look good externally.

This pressure is making dads give up money in the form of paid time off. "Millions of dads are leaving money and benefits on the table," says Heather Boushey, who works with both the Washington Center for Equitable Growth and the Center for American Progress. Put all that together and we're talking the equivalent of billions of dollars.

The case of Ariel Ayanna shows just how far these stigmas can go. He's the one-time rock star at his law firm whom I mentioned in the Introduction. "He by all reports did a wonderful job, more than met his hours, got a big bonus. Everything was going well," said Lori A. Jodoin, one of his attorneys, in describing the case to a group of colleagues in 2012.

Ariel's wife had mental-health issues that turned very serious. While pregnant with their second child, she attempted suicide. Ariel took a leave of absence under FMLA to care for her and the children. That was unheard of at his firm. Ariel broke with the firm's "macho" culture, he said in a court filing.

Ariel came back to work earlier than expected—after only eight weeks, though by law he could have taken twelve. But the firm "started monitoring and documenting his job performance," according to his attorney. He was assigned to be one person's assistant and was not reassigned to his previous client teams. Work was withheld from him. He was derided for being primary caregiver to his children. Four months later, the firm let him go, alleging that his "personal needs" got in the way of his work.

In a deposition, the firm's general counsel admitted that sex stereotyping was prevalent at the firm, Ariel's attorneys say. Men would brag about spending little time at home. One associate—who repeatedly "belittled" Ariel—referred to his own wife as "the princess." When Ariel was fired, that attorney was made a partner.

Ariel filed suit. A legal battle ensued, and a judge agreed to allow the case to go to trial, so a jury could consider whether the firm had illegally recriminated against him for using FMLA.

The firm argued that there was no recrimination. But the judge found that when the firm blamed Ayanna's "personal" issues for getting in the way of his work, a "reasonable jury could find that the comment was directed at Ayanna's recent need to take FMLA leave." Right before the trial was to begin in 2013, the firm settled.

The firm, Dechert LLP, declined comment for this book. Its website, with no mention of the case, announces big steps it has taken, including "increasing emphasis on work/life balance leading to a significant change in the firm's paid family leave policy. The firm increased paid leave for U.S. lawyers from twelve weeks to an industry-high of eighteen weeks and permits an additional eight weeks of unpaid leave." It also adopted "formal policies permitting partners, counsel, and associates—both men and women—to work part-time while raising children or taking care of other family members. These benefit programs extend to domestic partners."

Dechert engaged "a top diversity consultant to conduct a global assessment of all lawyers to understand their views of the firm," and it hosts "cultural competence seminars to increase the level of comfort and dialogue around the firm." The website also includes sections extolling the firm's "culture and core values," diversity, and a "global women's initiative." In addition, "the firm acknowledges that diverse lawyers may face unique challenges and diversity efforts intend to provide an additional layer of support," the website says.

Looks like someone got the message. At least on paper. And that's a critical distinction. Across the country, virtually all workplaces claim to be advanced, fair, and champions of diversity. Those claims are often fig leaves. That's why a recent *Harvard Business Review* study is so significant. It shows how bad things really are. The study found that men in C-suites by and large "still think of their family responsibilities in terms of breadwinning."[8] And even those "who pride themselves on having achieved some degree of balance between work and other realms of their lives measure themselves against a traditional male ideal. 'The ten minutes I give my kids at night is one million times greater than spending that ten minutes at work,' one interviewee said."[9]

Ten minutes? This anonymous executive is cheating himself and his family out of time together. They're missing moments that matter. Fatherhood isn't just about showing up to the recitals, games, and teacher conferences.

In a positive sign of the generational shift, the Harvard study reported that although "executives of both sexes consider the tension between work and family to be primarily a women's problem," the students who interviewed them "find that discouraging."[10]

As a nation, we've barely budged since one man made history in 1999 with the nation's first-ever sex discrimination verdict related to FMLA. Kevin Knussman is the Maryland state trooper I mentioned earlier, whose boss refused him the leave he was legally entitled to because, in her view, men aren't meant to care for children. A jury awarded him $375,000 for emotional damages.

These days, a growing phenomenon is throwing sexist bosses for a loop: two-dad families. When Andy Miller, of Austin, has told his bosses he needs to stay home to take care of his son, "I've never been met with anything other than, 'Okay, yeah, you need to do it.' Because I didn't have a wife at home."

His partner, Brian, has had a similar experience. When Andy's mother, who watches their son during the day, had to be hospitalized, Brian told his boss he needed to miss work. "The first response I got back was, 'Well, I'm sorry she's ill, but that doesn't mean you have to be gone.' And I was like, 'She keeps our kid.' I could see my boss recalibrate—something like, 'Oh yeah, he's gay.'" Now these same bosses need to learn that even men married to women can care for their children.

Have you seen these stigmas play out in your workplace? Whether you're a man or woman, and whether or not the stigma currently affects you, here are five steps to take:

1. Speak with a lawyer. Find out your rights and responsibilities in your state. Bring your lawyer a copy of the written rules of conduct that your employer has for all employees. Ideally you can have this initial conversation for a small fee or even free, with a lawyer friend or a nonprofit group such as the Center for WorkLife Law. (For resources, see the website for this book.)

2. Document. Keep very specific notes about everything you see or experience that reinforces the stigma. Who said what, and who was there?

3. Corroborate. Get written records of other people acknowledging what they saw as well. It can be as simple as an e-mail to a colleague saying, "Can you believe that so-and-so said, 'Blah, blah?'" When that colleague responds, you have written corroboration that it happened. Do this in a private e-mail or Facebook message from your home computer or phone, rather than your employer's e-mail system.

4. Speak with Human Resources. Have a meeting with the department concerned with this issue to explain what you have seen or experienced and why it concerns you. Mention that you have documented the problem and be sure to emphasize, in a friendly way, that before having this meeting you consulted with a lawyer so that you'd be aware of all your rights and responsibilities. Explain that you simply wanted to handle this difficult decision right. Immediately afterward, type out everything that was said in this meeting, in detail.

5. Offer to help. Some organizations and experts travel to workplaces and teach HR professionals how to adapt to the realities of modern families. Offer to help organize a trip for one of these groups to visit your workplace and hold a seminar. Speak in a positive way as a member of the team who wants to make things better, so that your employer will hold on to and attract top-notch workers.

Many employers may be glad you brought the issue forward before they found themselves embroiled in a lawsuit from someone hurt by the stigma. However, if your office punishes you for making your concerns known, you can take legal action. Discuss it with your attorney.

The increasing attention paid to this form of sexism is helping employers take notice. And fortunately, something happened in 2014 that gave America a wake-up call.

In Search of Neanderthals

The first week of April 2014, America changed for the better. No one saw it coming.

It started with a Major League Baseball player. Daniel Murphy, second baseman for the New York Mets, used one whole day of his three days of paternity leave to be home with his wife and newborn. To some clueless yakkers, this made Murphy a heathen. "Assuming the birth went well," New York sports radio host Craig Carton said, after twenty-four hours "you get your ass back to your team and you play baseball."

"There's nothing you can do anyway. You're not breastfeeding the kid," Carton added on his show, *Boomer & Carton,* which is also televised nationally. "I got four of these little rug rats. There's nothin' to do!"

His cohost, former NFL quarterback Boomer Esiason, somehow managed to get even more offensive. "I would've said, 'C-section before the season starts. I need to be at opening day,'" he declared.

Then, as though there was some weird competition to out-moron each other, another sports radio show host took things even farther. Mike Francesa, who has his own program, didn't just slam Daniel Murphy. He went after the entire concept of paternity leave, calling it "a scam and a half." He even called his own employer's offer of two weeks leave "ridiculous." "What do you need ten days for? What are you supposed to be doing? Vacationing?"

These comments spread like wildfire on social media. America could have rolled its collective eyes or just ignored it—or, worse, acted as though these love children of Archie Bunker and Ralph Kramden had a legitimate point. Instead, several news agencies reported on the offensive remarks. And those of us committed to ending the time-warp sexism fought back—and won.

I wrote an open letter to the radio hosts on my Tumblr blog. Perhaps a decade earlier it might have languished, barely read by anyone. But it spread quickly. The *Huffington Post* picked it up, putting it front and center in its Parents section. The *Shriver Report* posted it front and center as well. The *New York Daily News* quoted me.

Here's part of what I wrote:

Dear Boomer & Carton and Mike Francesa,

That's an incredible amount of ignorance you spewed. And it's shameful to men and women everywhere.

Your remarks . . . were so mind-bogglingly clueless, it's hard to believe they were real. SNL couldn't have scripted a better segment and called it "The Time-Traveling Sexists."

Where have you been for the last several decades, when America has revolutionized? Today's dads aren't just at the hospital for the births of our children. We're at home taking care of them, holding them, doing feedings (maybe you're unfamiliar with breast pumps and formula?), changing them, reading to them in those critical early days of their lives—days that form bonds and a system of caregiving that tremendously affects their lives and the balance of responsibilities men and women take on at home for years to come.

I could overwhelm you with studies and statistics to prove this, but based on the intellectual level of your comments, I'm pretty sure you wouldn't understand them. Or care. Especially given that you, Boomer & Carton, somehow decided there's a federal law requiring that men get two weeks' paternity leave. If you're going to make things up, why not at least pretend that moms get guaranteed paid leave? And your statement that Murphy and his wife should have scheduled a C-section based on his work schedule—who says that? Who thinks that? How much do you get paid for this moronic drivel?

"Get your ass back to work?" Seriously, was this some sort of delayed April Fools joke? . . .

The same goes for you, Mike. . . . Do you have any idea how offensive this is to both moms and dads? No, of course you don't.

I explained that these days it's getting harder to find "Neanderthals," which I defined as:

guys with their heads dug so far down in the sand (or elsewhere) that they've missed how America has evolved. There are incredibly few left, contrary to the stereotype. But thanks to the few with megaphones, like you, the stereotype remains alive and well.

It isn't too late for you to join the modern world. You can open your minds and learn. Reach out to me or to millions of other dads who can set you straight. In 2014, that would be the manly thing to do.[1]

I wasn't attacked for writing this. Instead, virtually all the responses were supportive. "Lovely op-ed, written by a grown-ass man," read one of my favorite tweets. Maria Shriver tweeted the letter to her millions of followers, saying, "Men need paternity leave."

"Boom! Josh Levs could just drop the mic and exit the stage," child psychologist Paula Bloom wrote on Facebook. "But I don't think he drops or exits when the work is so important." A women's group at

Columbia Journalism School thanked me and discussed the post at a conference.

Most important, dads and moms expressed their own outrage through social media and the traditional media. There were still, of course, a few hateful stragglers, including one guy who wrote me that he had just had a baby and agrees that ten days of paternity leave should never be offered, because men aren't needed at home.

Esiason, fifty-three, apologized. He said he had put Daniel Murphy and his wife in the midst of a public discussion that he "basically started by uttering insensitive comments."[2] No such statements from the other two radio hosts.

This ugly incident had turned into an opportunity. Americans galvanized to demonstrate that these dads, the stereotypes I referred to earlier, are the exceptions. The overwhelming majority of the country supports modern parenthood and its necessary corollary, paternity leave. "What's remarkable about Esiason's comment in hindsight is not the idiotic statement itself, but the monumental backlash to it and his subsequent apology," Jessica Grose wrote on *Slate*. "That players lobbied for and MLB put paternity leave in place is a positive step for pro sports. Even more heartening is that every time someone makes a snide remark about that leave, he gets shouted down."[3]

Murphy said that for his wife, who had an unscheduled C-section, "having me there helped a lot, and vice versa, to take some of the load off. . . . It felt, for us, like the right decision to make."[4]

Baseball is the only major league sport with paternity leave, and it just began in 2011. Texas Rangers' pitcher Colby Lewis was the first to take it, and he suffered some of the same criticism. But more and more players have followed suit—nearly one hundred by the time Murphy took his, and many more since.[5]

The Mets stood by Murphy. "When you start attacking Dan Murphy's credibility, you need to look in the mirror a little bit," said manager Terry Collins. He added that "there's nothing wrong" with taking paternity leave.[6] "The birth of a child is a once in a lifetime event," said first baseman Josh Satin, and although games "are very important, family should come first."[7]

So even in the world of professional all-male sports, this important change is under way. Neanderthals are not representative of the masses.

Now, a crucial caveat. None of this makes light of how much sexism still exists in America, much of it—unlike the simple stupidity of the radio hosts—horrifying and dangerous. In my work, I cover domestic violence, sexual assault, murders, and all sorts of other events that highlight the twisted, depraved depths of sexism. I see the seedier parts of the Internet, the intrusions of privacy, the hacking of private photos, the objectification of women. The good dads of America—the vast majority of fathers in this country—must lead the way in fighting against all forms of sexism, both the idiotic and the barbaric. It's essential that we do this. We need to drown it out. There's power in numbers.

It's the same power that all of us parents, both moms and dads, must harness to bring about fair policies. That requires all of us to give something up, though—something we just might preach against, but secretly like.

Male Privilege, Female Gatekeeping, and the Bonus Temptation

Male privilege is a hard thing to let go of." That's what Keith Cunningham-Parmeter says of why many men aren't taking even the paid paternity leave they're offered. "Today we hear descriptions of modern, 'involved' fathers who want to trade wages for family time to play more active roles in their children's lives," Keith wrote in a report called "Men at Work, Fathers at Home."

"In reality, though, most men pay mere lip service to such ideals, 'talking the talk' about equal caregiving, but failing to alter their work patterns in ways that actually create more time for child care," he writes. Keith credits "a few men" with offering "an alternative model. These fathers resist cultural expectations that result in uninvolved fathering. They spend more time with their children than fathers have at any time since experts began measuring male caregiving."[1]

On much of this, I disagree. As I've established, numerous studies show that fathers in general are committed to being all in as parents, spending substantial time with their children. The "few men" are those dads who don't make the effort to be home with their families. But when it comes to paternity leave, does he have a point? Are some dads—maybe even many—avoiding it because they want to?

Are we as men giving in to stigmas and avoiding the battles it would take to get substantial paternity leave, because this way we're off the hook? Maybe we think it's just easier to say, "Sorry, honey, no choice—I have to go to work."

"It's a matter of holding onto power as long as you can," Keith said in an interview. "Why would you give up the benefits of pay, job, privilege, and prestige when you can conveniently skirt that, leaving the caregiving to someone else?"

"Because you pay a price for that privilege," I countered. "Ultimately, as a dad, you're missing out."

He agreed, but said that on some level many men are afraid of what it will mean for them if they give up "male privilege." Gender stigmas aren't just external, Keith said. Many dads have bought into them. They worry that taking the time off might actually mean "doing something feminine."

"I can speak from my experience," he went on. "I live in Portland, Oregon, which should be this utopia of men and women holding hands and all sharing everything. And to some degree it is. I'm involved in the PTA. I just biked my kids to school. I made lunches. But dads like me are still a distinct minority."

Keith believes change is coming. Dads who want to hold on to that privilege will find "their hands are going to be forced. The economy is equalizing a lot of this," he says. With women getting the majority of college degrees, Americans will find "it's expensive for a country to offload all its domestic labor duties on its more educated workforce. Employers are going to realize that, and American couples are going to realize that they've got to maximize their earning potential—and for employers, their talent pool." In other words, more highly educated women will have the ability to make more money, so it'll make sense for more men to stay home. And that'll help push reluctant dads, while also pushing employers to establish fair policies.

There's no way to know or quantify to what extent Keith may be right about dads "talking the talk." Given the level of work-life conflicts we're experiencing, it seems most men really want to walk the walk. We want to be home more for child rearing. Still, Keith makes an important point: moving forward in this fight for equality means sacrificing this "privilege." But it means gaining a lot more—more paid time off with our kids, better lives for our wives and ourselves, and more equality for our sons and daughters when they enter the workforce someday. Step one in this effort is for dads to start using every day of paid paternity leave that they're given and to fight back if they're punished in any way.

But there's also another reason many men don't use their paid paternity-leave days. We want to feel useful and needed. That's why Richard Dorment, of *Esquire,* declined his company's paid leave and returned to work a few days after his son's birth. "It's not because I was scared about appearing weak to my mostly male coworkers or employers, and it's not because I was any more wary of losing my job than usual," he wrote in the magazine. "At work, I had a purpose—things needed to be done, people needed me to do them. At home, watching my wife feed and swaddle our son and then retreat to our bed to get some sleep of her own, I learned what many first-time fathers learn: assuming an absence of any health issues related to child or mother, the first six weeks of a child's life are fairly uneventful for men."[2]

His column angered some people. Writer Rebecca Greenfield of *The Wire* slammed Dorment for "suggesting men shouldn't take paternity leave because women hog all the parenting work at the outset."[3]

Dorment says his "very active mother-in-law" contributed to his decision. "I didn't feel like standing around, being somebody who went out to run errands. I like feeling useful, I like feeling needed. So I went to work to do that."

Unlike the radio Neanderthals, Dorment doesn't insult or oppose the idea of paternity leave. He supports its existence. And his experience does speak for some other men. There are couples in which, for various reasons, the mom—sometimes with the help of her own mother—decides to do just about everything with the newborn. Men can be made to feel irrelevant in the initial weeks after a birth.

It's still hard for me or many other dads to imagine an "uneventful" first few weeks. And although couples have the right to make their own choices, I would never accept being tossed out as unneeded in the initial weeks of my child's life. Even if my wife wanted to do everything alone, I'd say, "Hell, no!" I'd take the baby between feedings, hold her, read to her, change her, take her for walks.

In some families, that's a tough thing to do because of another issue that's sensitive but important to talk about: maternal gatekeeping. "As women must be more empowered at work, men must be more empowered at home," Sheryl Sandberg writes in *Lean In*. "I have seen so many women inadvertently discourage their husbands from doing their share by being too controlling or critical. Social scientists call this 'maternal gatekeeping,' which is a fancy term for 'Ohmigod, that's not the way you do it! Just move aside and let me!'" Moms have "great power to encourage or impede the fathers' involvement," Sandberg says.[4]

As men, we understand where this comes from, and it's natural that we'd want to show some deference. After your wife has carried the baby for nine months and gone through the painful, amazing, miraculous throes of childbirth, of course she would be protective. Still, as dads we need to assert our equality—for the betterment of our wives as much as for ourselves. Often when my wife starts telling me how to do something, I say, "Okay, gatekeeper!" We laugh, and she suddenly remembers that I don't need instructions. One day I was sitting next to someone we're close to as he held our baby, a new experience for him. My wife came over to try to reposition her or take her away, and his wife was watching him intently the whole time, as though he had to perform and prove his abilities to her. "Go away! We're good here," I said, laughing. Our wives smiled and left him alone.

A guy can't help all that much through pregnancy, although as dads we try. But after the birth, once the baby's home, we have the chance to tell our wives, "We can both take it from here."

"When our first child was born, my wife went through all the typical anxieties that new moms go through, combined with the guilt of being away periodically," because she travels for work, Nate, in Indianapolis, told me. "That started to manifest itself in 'micromanaging' how I took care of our daughter. I explained how she was coming across, which wasn't her intent. And I just didn't provide as much information, so she wouldn't get into every detail. It wasn't about keeping things from her, but more about focusing her on things she really needed to know versus getting her in the weeds. Frankly, I learned this from how our babysitter interacted with me. Those two actions pretty much solved the situation. It took some months to find the right balance, but we got it to work and have ever since."

Washington attorney Shaun Leighton says that as his wife's career has progressed and become more demanding, "It's challenged her ideas about my role in the family." Still, she "hasn't learned how to accept my help. She may want me to do things, and I'll do them my way. It may not be what she wanted. That's part of the balance we're trying to find now. It's very much a work in progress."

In covering fatherhood, I've often used the phrase "Dads do it differently." I've looked at how men and women get the same tasks accomplished in different ways, equally well. "She drove me crazy with the pattern of the sheets and how to decorate the room," Josh Azriel says of his wife, Michelle, laughing. "I'd rather watch the game than go over patterns. To me they all look alike." Michelle loves that he doesn't care about things like that, and Josh loves that she does.

Michelle credits that difference with helping save her sanity and her health in the early days of raising Mia, the baby they adopted after years of trying to conceive. "I'm anxious by nature," Michelle says, curled up on the sofa next to Josh. "You have to take care of yourself, and I did not do a good job at that." She was worrying over every little thing with Mia and insisting that she take care of all those things herself.

"If you lose a lot of sleep, you tend to go a little wacky," Josh says. "I went to my next-door neighbor, who has two kids, and I said, 'I'm gonna take Mia to the grocery store. You've got to go knock on our door and pretend you're just coming by to say hi. You've got to talk to my wife. She's not resting. She won't listen to what anyone has to say.'"

That did the trick. Bringing people in to talk to her was "one of the best things" Josh did for her, Michelle says. Her days as an obsessive gatekeeper came to an end.

Both these problems—male privilege and female gatekeeping—exist not just inside some homes, but also in public. Just as Ariel Ayanna had male colleagues who showed off about not doing much at home, some women continue gatekeeping wherever they go. "I am policed when I am in public in a way that my wife is not," says Keith Cunningham-Parmeter. "I will let the kids push the cart or sit in the cart where the groceries are supposed to go. And I have had women try and tell me, 'Be careful. Your kid's going to get hurt.' And I'm like, 'Thank you very much. Mind your own business. I can watch my kids.'"

Most dads experience this. I've had women try to tell me I'm holding my child wrong or that I shouldn't let one of my kids do something. I remind myself that they're trying to help. "I've got this," I say, and walk away.

The flip side of this is when strangers make a big deal of dads being out with their kids, as though somehow that's an unusual sight. Facebook executive Tom Stocky rails against "the ridiculous praise" he often gets for changing a diaper or buying groceries with his daughter. While on paternity leave, he learned to hate the "backhanded compliments," such as, "Your wife must work so hard. It's great that you're able to pick up the slack."[5]

"Has someone ever said that to a woman?" Stocky asked in a Facebook post.[6] Even people with the best intentions can reinforce sexist expectations and stereotypes and send the message to the children hearing those comments that child care is still "women's work."

To be fair, there surely are rare cases when gatekeeping by a mom or dad can make sense. If one parent is incredibly clumsy or irresponsible, the other parent has reason to be protective. Then again, ideally someone who can't handle a baby wouldn't have one—or would develop those skills before the birth.

Andy Miller went out one night and left his baby, Clark, with his own father, who had been absent for most of Andy's childhood. "When we came home, my dad was asleep on the couch and Clark was asleep in his crib. I told my mother that, and she wigged out. She flipped. She was like, 'What do you mean you left the baby with him?!'"

Andy discovered it may have been a first for his father. "My mom wouldn't allow it. The first three years of my life she says I was never left alone with my dad—ever. I don't think he thought anything of it." Not knowing what Andy's dad was like back then, we can't know whether that was a rare case in which maternal gatekeeping kept a kid safe.

These days, fortunately, you rarely hear of an extreme situation like that. Still, male privilege and maternal gatekeeping can pull us into more traditional patterns and prevent us from achieving parental equality. It takes something powerful to help us avoid those traps.

Other parts of the world have found a solution. It's what I'm calling the Bonus Temptation. "Some countries offer a bonus of family leave only if men take it," Keith says. Sometimes it's as much as two months paid. "The rate of men taking leave has gone from literally the single digits to 80 or 90 percent in these countries. I've never seen a public policy flip behavior this much."

The Bonus Temptation reverses the stigma. When it's two full months of use-it-or-lose-it paid time, men look ridiculous for turning it down. "The families aren't stupid," Keith says. "The wife or partner says, 'You'd better take your frickin' leave!'"

This is another strong argument for substantial amounts of paid parental leave for American men. A couple of weeks are easier to pass up. But giving up six or eight weeks of paid leave to take care of your child? That's downright crazy.

We can make this happen. Some businesses will start doing the right thing the more we as Americans ask them to. But in some cases legal action will be needed. That's why you need to know the three letters that are changing the legal landscape.

The New Legal Front Line

FRD

I n late 2012, a group of four women, all lawyers, in different parts of the country held a private conference call. Together, they mapped out how to win the legal battle for dads in the workplace.

The conversation, recorded and provided to me exclusively for this book with the approval of the participants, focused on "family responsibilities discrimination," referred to among these lawyers by its acronym, FRD. This may be the first time you've seen the term, but it won't be the last. It's the new front line.

The four women spoke about the importance of encouraging more men to bring forward claims when they experience sex discrimination. Attorneys are still longing for the big one—a case that will make it through trial and succeed, establishing a court precedent and capturing the nation's attention. "There's no perfect Title VII case on point for gender stereotyping of a male caregiver right now," employment attorney Stephanie Bornstein said in the phone conference. "That's going to change with the folks on this call."

When caregivers take legal action over discrimination at work, they usually follow one of two paths. Some file FMLA claims—complaints that their workplaces retaliated against them for taking

leave that they're legally entitled to. Others file sex discrimination cases arguing that their employers treated them unfairly based on traditional assumptions about how men and women will or should behave as caregivers.

Attorney Cynthia Calvert, who led the call, described a case that was in the news. A San Francisco city official was accused of demoting men after they took two weeks of paternity leave. One employee filed suit alleging that the official retaliated against him for taking paternity leave. But "very typically, he did not file a claim for sex discrimination," Calvert lamented. To lawyers fighting this battle, that's a big error. It's tantamount to shooting yourself in the foot before beginning a race. As long as the facts support it, the best move is to pursue both of these legal options, she said.

Bornstein gave a couple of examples of FRD victims. One was a truck driver who lived with and cared for his eighty-seven-year-old mother. "His coworkers posted graphic drawings depicting him as gay or transsexual. Really, really disturbing stuff around the workplace repeatedly. That was the harassment piece of it. When he complained, his employer agreed that it was wrong, but then retaliated against him by giving him less work and targeting him for discipline. Ultimately, he had to take a leave to care for his mother, and he was fired while he was on the leave."

In another case, Bornstein said, "A man who was doing an outstanding job as a sales representative took one day off to help his pregnant girlfriend find a doctor. He was then told by his boss that he basically had to decide if he wanted to totally commit himself to this endeavor, and that he wasn't going to tolerate working with a guy who didn't give it his all." The boss said he would monitor the employee's work closely and that "if he didn't want to work under that kind of scrutiny, he should leave."

These are the kinds of cases that could succeed if they make it to a jury. But many judges don't allow them to go that far. "Courts are really having trouble recognizing sex discrimination against hetero-sexual men," Bornstein said. "The real problem here is a failure to recognize the masculine gender stereotype in the context of bread-winning and caregiving, because it is such a deeply entrenched norm in our society." And very often, potential FRD cases aren't even filed in the first place, because many workers and lawyers aren't aware that it's an option, Calvert says.

So why do these cases fare better at trial? Because companies don't understand FRD laws either, Calvert says. "They don't understand the magnitude of their exposure. And so a lot of them are not settling when they should be settling."

The more men step forward, the more cases will succeed. And companies will get the message. So lawyers like Cynthia Calvert and Joan Williams are very happy to see that they're getting more calls than ever from dads.

And there's more good news. Some states, cities, and towns are coming up with their own FRD laws. "This is an absolute game changer," says Calvert. The way some of these laws are written, you don't have to prove sex discrimination in order to prove family respon-sibility discrimination—so it's easier to claim and prove. "San Francisco passed a provision that you can't discriminate based on family status—it's huge. Washington, D.C., says you can't have family responsibilities discrimination—that's pretty much ideal, and we'd like to move every-one toward that. Alaska says you can't discriminate based on parental status. We have cities around the country—Chicago, Cambridge, some big and also some very small places, towns that have just thirty thou-sand people. It's wonderful. That helps so much more."

The laws aren't perfect, she says. "Some apply to an employer who has only four employees. Others say you have to have fifteen or twenty. Some allow employees to go to court for it. Others say no, it has to be the human-relations agency for the county that hears the charges and awards the damages. So it's sort of all over the place."

Still, Calvert and other activists are pushing other jurisdictions around the country to adopt similar laws and to define "family responsibilities" not just as caring for a child, but caring for any family member. They also want a federal law to "provide uniformity for employers" on what they can and can't do legally.

Keith Cunningham-Parmeter says the solution is to amend Title VII to make caregiver status an officially protected class. "Your status as a caregiver couldn't be considered when making hiring and firing decisions, promotion and demotion decisions, transfer decisions. For example, let's say you have a new position that requires a lot of travel. You're the employer and you've got one applicant with young kids and another who's childless. They're both go-getters. You think they're both great, but you're like, 'Yeah, I think the woman with three kids is gonna miss some of these trips. She's gonna have sick kids, and she's gonna be the one staying home, because the husband's not gonna do it.'

"Right now that's potentially legal. It could be family responsibilities discrimination, but you'd have to prove sex discrimination. But if you say that parenthood just can't be considered, it makes it easier for people to win those kinds of claims."

Of course, it's critical to know that when you're applying for a job, employers can't ask for personal information. You're not required to even mention having children. But if you feel that you have options—that the company really wants you, but you don't *need* that particular job—feel free to ask questions about things like flexibility and corporate culture. And pose those questions to trustworthy contacts inside the company who can tell you what it's really like.

So FRD laws are an important part of the battle ahead. But since so few cases make it to trial, it will require a lot more dads who are willing to fight for fairness. The task now for American men and women, on this front, boils down to one thing.

Rise Up

A friend jolted me with a single sentence. A fellow dad, he had called about my case and was emotional, tearing up. "When's the last time a man stood up for his family?"

We don't see or hear a lot about men doing this, but some are. As you've heard, men like Ariel Ayanna, Kevin Knussman, and Jay Ramsay stood up in important ways. So did Mark McNulty, a teacher in Boston who took on his school. As I mentioned in the Introduction, he decided to take two years off and have his job held. Superiors then informed him that offer was only supposed to apply to women, even though the contract used no gender-specific language. Mark challenged the policy and, so far, has been managing to take the time off—apparently with his job still held. So he's a pioneer in his district.

Still, these examples are too few and far between. And understandably so. Who wants to risk his career and face ridicule by taking on backward policies and stigmas?

More men might be willing to if they knew their rights. My experience has shown me that incredibly few workers in this country are aware of the laws that protect them. Some attorneys are unaware as well. Since I took on Time Warner, numerous lawyers have asked me to explain the EEOC process to them. One very smart lawyer I know even said to me, "Men aren't protected against gender bias."

"Yes, they are," I responded. "Of course, we are!"

He thought for a moment and then said, "Oh, yeah, I guess so."

Even lawyers who know these laws will often feel that a case is not worth pursuing, says Cynthia Calvert. "It can be very expensive. And if you're not going to get a lot on the other end, then that limits this kind of effort to only rich guys. A lot of employment lawyers are not taking cases on a contingency anymore. It's very hard for poor employees to get representation."

Calvert and her counterpart, Joan Williams, are helping change that. They train attorneys and investigators at the EEOC to spot legitimate legal claims. And they run sessions for other lawyers, explaining that judgments can be large enough to make the fight worth their time.

But rising up isn't just about legal action. It's a matter of using all the platforms at our disposal—news stories, websites, social media, public events, town halls, council meetings, and more—to speak out.

Keith Cunningham-Parmeter compares today's caregiving discrimination to sexual harassment, which "was accepted behavior as recently as the 1970s, maybe early 1980s. It was through advocacy, public policy, education, and litigation that now any HR department is scared to death of any hint of sexual harassment in the workplace."

"What fathers are doing is still flying below the radar in our culture," says Brad Harrington, executive director of the Center for Work and Family. "And to some degree, organizational culture and peers at work encourage it to stay beneath the radar."

Dads can change that by joining the public conversations on gender issues, sharing experiences, and amplifying the arguments women have been making. Women can help by making sure men are welcomed into these conversations with open arms and minds. "As dads we feel we're not really allowed to complain in the public sphere," says Michael Kress, who until mid-2014 was editor of Parents.com, "because if we do, moms can say, 'We have it worse.'" He adds, "It doesn't have to be a competition. We all have challenges in our lives."

Stay-at-home dad Chris Routly feels that as women "have become

more free in the workplace, there has not been an equivalent movement in the other direction. It's not just that men didn't push themselves. They weren't welcomed."

This is why my experience getting so much support in the fight for
fair paternity leave is so important. It proves that men are welcomed
with open arms into these conversations. Ready to take action to fight
for fair parental leave policies? Here are the top ten steps all of us—
men and women—can take:

1. *Investigate* the policies where you work, down to the most
extreme specifics. Read all the language your HR department
can provide.

2. *Learn the protocol* for requesting a change quietly from
within. Ask your HR representative how an employee can go
about requesting a policy change. You're under no obligation
to announce this to your own manager unless the protocol
specifically calls for it.

3. *Lawyer up.* Consult a good attorney with an excellent
track record on issues involving gender discrimination in the
workplace. The Center for WorkLife Law offers a hotline you
can call. If you meet with an attorney in your area, you should
not have to pay more than a nominal fee, if anything, for an
initial consultation. Learn your rights, which depend on the
state in which you live.

4. *Research.* Using information you find in this book, information you might learn from friends in similar businesses, and
guidance from a good attorney, compile notes to prepare a
positive presentation for your HR department. Operate on the
assumption that your employer will choose to do the right thing.

5. *Present your proposal,* either in person or in writing, depending on what's allowed and how you best express yourself. Be

very positive, but also confident in your messaging. If you have a specific time frame by which you need an answer—for example, if you have a baby on the way—explain this.

6. *Build a team (optional).* If you have colleagues you trust who are confident enough to join you in this quest, get them involved. Sometimes there's power in numbers. Still, keep your communication in writing so you have a record. You don't want an unscrupulous colleague, whom you thought you could trust, violating your confidence. If colleagues support you, recommend that they express this in a positive way to HR as well.

7. *Document.* Keep written records of absolutely everything— and not just in your work e-mail, which your employer can close you out of. Save all these written communications in a private e-mail, cloud storage, or even printed out in hard copies.

If you get the response you wanted from your employer, great! You're done. If not, or if you get no response and it's getting close to your deadline:

8. *Discuss options* with your attorney. If he or she seems scared or reluctant to make a move, consult another attorney. Ask lots of questions based on what you've read in this book. Give them a copy of this book! And consult nonprofit legal groups that might be there to support you. After I announced my case, numerous legal experts and groups contacted me, including the ACLU.

9. *Make your choice—with conviction.* With excellent legal advice, think through each possible scenario, and ultimately go with what your gut tells you. Remember that if you file with the EEOC, you have protections—including from recrimination by your employer. If your employer does take action against you illegally, you can sue.

10. Summon the courage and confidence to do what's right. Know that if you do, there will be men and women ready to support you. As dads, we still have an especially strong sense that providing financially is the most important thing we can do for our families. It isn't. Showing your children how to stand up and fight for fairness—in a smart, determined way—is more important than giving them an iPad or taking them on costly vacations.

If you're up for an eleventh step, contact me through the website for this book. I'd love to hear about your case.

All of this is essential if you're going to fight for fair family-leave policies. But it's only one piece of the puzzle. To build a work culture that values families, men and women need to rise up against the rest of the anachronistic structures holding all of us back.

PART II

Beyond Leave

Fixing the Struggle Between Work and Life

Flexibility

How to Reshape Your Work Life

When Bryan Levey became a dad, he decided he was going to start working only four days a week and not extend each day beyond eight hours. He was vice president of engineering for a successful Boston-area technology company, at which that was unheard of. Stunned colleagues declared him "lucky." "You can do it too. You just have to have a plan," he told them. You'd think that as a top executive he'd be expected to put in incredible hours at least five days a week, if not six. But Bryan kept a promise he had made to himself. "Shortly after I started my career, my dad got colon cancer and died a year later. It was pivotal for me. My parents' relationship was very strong and very traditional. She stayed home, but one role was not more important than the other. I remember their always talking about how they were going to travel when they retired. It was heartbreaking for me that, the year before my father was going to retire, he passed away. My mom soldiered on and traveled, but it wasn't the same.

"I said to myself, 'That's not going to be me.' I remember telling my boss during our wedding toast, 'I used to work all the time, but now I have someone who's important to me.' It was clear I wanted to balance these things."

Bryan's wife, Lisa, an organizational development consultant, helped him break the work addiction and move in the right direction. Before they had children, Bryan and Lisa spent six weeks vacationing in Europe. Those six weeks may have proved particularly fruitful. Nine months later, their first child was born. By the time their baby boy arrived, Bryan had spoken to people at work about the new schedule he wanted to follow. He also took off six weeks after the birth, unpaid.

"This was my first ah-ha moment," he says. "Monday would be day care; Tuesday, Daddy Day; Wednesday, day care; Thursday, Mommy Day; Friday, day care."

Bryan was fortunate to have been able to make this kind of decision. "I felt like I had job security. I'd been with the company since I got out of college, seven or eight years. At this point I was a leader. I said, 'I'll make sure it works,' and they trusted that I would."

He also gave the company a big incentive to let him try this. Bryan agreed to work for 80 percent of his salary. "I took that pay cut. I said, 'I'm not working ten-hour days, even though sometimes I did end up doing that. But if I had requested four ten-hour days, I would have wound up doing twelve hours sometimes."

For his office, it was a winning proposition. "I found out I could get just as much work done in four days as five, because when I was home I was thinking about home and when I was at work I was thinking about work. You don't need to throw in extra time at work; you just need to be focused," Bryan says.

He and Lisa now have two boys. The oldest is eighteen; the other in middle school. After nine years at the shorter schedule, he switched back to a five-day week. "But it continues to be a consistent goal of mine to balance work and home. I generally am home for after-school homework at least once a week at 3:00 and get the kids ready in the morning two or three times a week. I plan on getting back to a four-day schedule soon."

A couple of years ago, he took off eight weeks for a big family summer trip. "If you plan ahead and make sure your responsibilities are taken care of, people won't even know you're gone," he says. "When I got back, the team said, 'You're back already?'"

Ivan Axelrod, COO of Provident Financial Management in Santa Monica, might have an even better deal. He works four days a week and took no pay cut. Again, it was unheard of at his company.

Ivan didn't do it for his children. He did it for his grandchildren. "I had a typical career path. My wife stayed home, because thirty years ago that was what people did," he says. But when his first granddaughter was born, he wanted to have a relationship with her and wanted her to know him. Ivan says, "My father passed away when both my children were very young, and they don't have any memories of their grandparents. I didn't want that to happen. Then I had to figure out how to do that, because I had an executive position. I decided the most important thing for me was to live for my children and grandchildren. So I worked out an arrangement with my partners." In addition to changing his schedule, he restructured his department, promising that it would deliver similar or even better results afterward.

Ivan offered to do some work from home during that fifth day, but it would not be a formal workday. His primary role that day would be caring for his granddaughter—a crucial help to his daughter when she went back to work. "My son-in-law had a full-time job as well. When I said I'd take one day a week, they looked at me like I was crazy!" Ivan's wife took one day a week as well, as did the third living grandparent.

Seven years later, Ivan is still doing this. He now cares for both his grandchildren. "I take her and her five-year-old brother to school. I park at the far end of the parking lot, and we walk to her classroom. And at seven, she continues to hold my hand. It gives me tremendous satisfaction to think of the bond we have between us. I know that's there forever."

He also feels good about helping his daughter and son-in-law develop their careers. His daughter recently got a substantial promotion.

And Ivan's business "hasn't really missed a beat," he says. Making this
family commitment helped him "push down responsibility" to those
who reported directly to him, allowing them to grow and flourish.

Ivan is working to instill this flexibility into his company. "We have
eighty people in my office. Maybe 75 percent are women. I have some
pushback from partners, because they're very traditional, saying everyone has to be here all the time—because when we were starting out,
we had to be here all the time. I've been able to make some progress
and assist others who want to do something similar."

Shaun Leighton is doing the same at the Washington law firm
where he is COO. He saw how well paternity leave and flexibility have worked for his family. Now he reports, "We've got a lot of
partners with younger children. Almost all of them are flexing their
schedules."

Bryan, Ivan, and Shaun are all involved with the ThirdPath Institute, a Philadelphia-based national nonprofit that helps "individuals,
families, and organizations in finding new ways to redesign work to
create time for family, community, and other life priorities." Men and
women looking to make a change call the agency for advice, direction, ideas, and resources.

Businesses are inching forward in offering flexible hours to more
workers.[1] But there's also a bad trend under way: flexibility involving
reduced time is *decreasing*.[2] And very few men are pursuing any kind
of formal arrangement. Even among the dads who take paternity
leave, only 6 percent negotiate a formal flexible work arrangement
afterward.[3]

More dads are working out informal arrangements. Ryan Miller
is one of them. He's executive editor of two weekly California newspapers. He and his wife, Sarah, who works with special-needs kids,
have three children. They don't want to hand the kids off to day care.
The two oldest are now in school, but the youngest is a toddler. "We
like a parent to be with him. My wife would love to not work and
stay home with the kids, but we can't afford it where we live," he told

me. "I recently picked up a second job. I write web copy at night for plastic surgeons."

Fortunately, Ryan's newspaper office is "pretty flexible," he says. Make that exceptionally flexible, given what he goes on to describe: "Sometimes I bring my son to work. I strap him onto me in a carrier. I'll walk around the newsroom, I'll walk around the block to do interviews on my phone. I don't have my own office. Sometimes I'm on the phone, thinking, 'How can I keep the interview subject from hearing this kid?' I'll shove graham crackers in his mouth, anything to keep him quiet."

No one wants an office full of babies or graham cracker bits bedecking the floors (at least no one I know), but we need more parents like Ryan to become bosses at work—people who understand modern parenthood—because many people who try to work out informal arrangements are running into brick walls. My wife experienced this. She was offered a job with an organization that's all about "thinking green." She presented the company with three scenarios that would work for her schedule. One involved being in the office more than thirty hours a week and doing the rest of her work at home. She even offered to put in a little more than forty hours a week total. They said no, prizing willingness to sit in an office an additional few hours over all the reasons they had selected her for the position. It was a disappointment to her and a loss to the company.

Her experience is common. Half of working parents have turned down a job that they felt would conflict with family obligations. The vast majority of workers want their companies to offer flexibility, and nearly six in ten working parents believe they'd do their jobs better if they were allowed a flexible schedule.[4]

A national debate on this exploded when Yahoo CEO Marissa Mayer announced in 2013 that telecommuting would no longer be allowed. Writer Lisa Belkin, a prominent voice on these issues, declared it "the exact opposite of what CEOs should be doing."[5] Jennifer Owens, editorial director of Working Mother Media, is quoted as calling it "a step backwards," in a *Forbes* article entitled "Back to the Stone Age?"[6]

Inc. magazine listed it, along with Mayer's introduction of a bell curve for employees' performance ratings, as the "top HR fail" of the year.[7] Number two on that list was what Time Warner did to me. (Number three was Lady Gaga's not paying her assistant overtime. So I was sandwiched between Marissa Mayer and Lady Gaga.)

Mayer said the best move for Yahoo at the time was to bring all employees together, and that her canceling telecommuting should not be perceived as "industry narrative." Still, workers throughout the country were legitimately worried about what Mayer's decision would signal. If a tech company like Yahoo wouldn't allow that kind of flexibility, why would theirs?

The benefits to businesses have been proven time and again. Telecommuters are almost twice as likely to put in more than forty hours a week, are more productive with creative tasks (though slightly less productive with repetitive work), and save their businesses and themselves thousands of dollars a year.[8] Seven in ten workers say telecommuting is an important benefit when considering a new job. Ten percent say they'd even take a pay cut.[9]

Lack of work flexibility is, sadly, something many American workers have become used to. But it's hurting us. It's one of the biggest things making today's family life so overextended. In a survey about the difficulties of balancing work and home life, dads said the biggest problem is the tremendous pressure to provide financially. The second biggest: "My job is not flexible enough about where and when to work."[10] (Men telecommute slightly more often than women, but parents don't telecommute any more often than nonparents.)[11]

Some offices might be willing to offer flexibility if only more of us asked. About half the nation's businesses say they periodically allow workers to change their hours. But less than a third of full-time workers say their businesses have that kind of flexibility. Why the difference? The White House says it could be that some businesses "would be willing to accommodate the needs of individual workers, but these workers are not aware of it."[12]

Still, there is a danger in asking, particularly for men. Researchers call it the "flexibility stigma." It's a type of "femininity stigma," attorney Joan Williams says. More than a third of working parents believe they've been passed over for a promotion, raise, or new job due to the need for a flexible work schedule.[13]

We need to rise up against the stigma. So it's worth it to ask, suggest, and even push for the flexibility you need. As workers, we have power. We are in demand. Many of us forgot this in the 2008 financial fiasco. If we have skills and are good at what we do, employers need us—not just vice versa. They have good reason to respond to the needs of real modern families. Let's show them what those needs are. Sure, we can get shot down. But sometimes we'll find businesses ready to change.

And if they don't respond favorably, we can look for workplaces that do. Jeff Porzio left one of the top advertising agencies for a smaller, less "bureaucratic" one. "Now, if I'm coaching my kid's basketball team, I don't think twice," he says. "It's their culture. You still know if someone's being productive or not via their laptops, and so on. You're always reachable. If I need to take vacation time, I take it with a clear conscience. I'm very lucky, and I reward the company with my loyalty."

Some men have turned to Mom Corps, a staffing firm that was created to place mothers in flexible positions around the country. "At least 10 percent of our database is now men," says founder Allison Karl O'Kelly. "We place a ton of them."

One is Scott Richey, of Fort Worth, Texas, a sales manager who needed more flexible work. He's now running national sales for a rapidly growing company while raising a son with his wife. "It was great to be able to find a new position that allowed me to maintain my family obligations and work a schedule that was beneficial to us both," he told Mom Corps.[14]

Some dads have found that launching their own business was the answer. Mark Garcia, a chef in San Antonio, Texas, didn't have much choice. He's raised his daughter alone since she was five. "When I filed for custody, I was an executive for a restaurant company and knew I would have to change my life. We had offices in New York and Texas. I couldn't travel like that. I opened a consulting agency, working with sports stars, chefs, and restaurateurs."

With much of his business coming from corporations, he was expected to travel at times. So he did something that, at the time, no other man he knew had done. He informed his clients that he would always need advance notice if they needed him to travel. Some clients were taken aback. "That's understandable to people if it comes from a woman, but there's a disconnect when it's the dad," he says.

Fortunately, flexibility seems to be an inevitable wave of the future. Younger employees rank it high in importance when choosing jobs. "Organizations that can offer more flexibility around reduced time, caregiving leaves, and flex careers will have a competitive edge in recruiting and retaining employees as the aging workforce and dual focus on personal and professional lives among younger employees become increasingly important drivers in the labor market," the Families and Work Institute says.[15]

But based on the current trajectory, it will take far too long to get where we need to go. "We're making strides. Even five, ten years ago you wouldn't have talked about flexibility on the job," says O'Kelly. "Still, I think this is something so ingrained in our culture and companies that it will take until our millennials are our CEOs for it to really take place."

Not if we take action now. Here are the top five steps we can take:

1. *Learn* your employer's policies on flexible schedules and telecommuting. Find out about any other employees who have used these options. Also speak with people in positions similar

to yours at similar companies—including, and especially, competitor agencies.

2. *Ask* your manager about the possibility of telecommuting and/or starting a flexible schedule. Remember you are not required to share any personal information.

3. *Design and present a pitch* for the type of schedule that would work for you. Just as with parental leave, present this pitch either in person or in writing, depending on how your employer operates and how you communicate best. In the pitch, explain how you would get your work done, be accessible when needed, and ensure results. Use information and data in this book. Use this pitch even if your manager has said there's no willingness to consider flexibility. You might change the company's mind!

4. *Set a time frame.* You might not get an answer the next day or the next week. Explain in the kindest way possible that you need to know by a certain date because of developments in your private life. Make it clear you're not threatening anything; you just need to plan.

5. The fifth step depends on the results you get:

> *a. Take it.* If you're given even just a bit of what you asked for, take it! You can show how well it works and be a pioneer. Fulfill all your work responsibilities and be prepared to show the results. Other employees will be jealous of you and may snark. Don't stoop to their level. Ignore the naysayers, and deliver results. Remember, you are standing up for your family and carving a path for others.

> *b. Look elsewhere.* If your employer refuses, look elsewhere for a job. Explain to prospective employers that this is a big

reason you're willing to make the move. Remember, you're
an American with a freedom that previous generations
fought and died for. Use it! Don't be afraid to go somewhere
in which the leadership respects and tries to accommodate
you as a modern, committed parent.

When people ask me about my fight for paternity-leave fairness,
I emphasize that there are all sorts of ways to rise up. So maybe you
can't take your employer to the EEOC for a sexist policy. Something
you can do, however, is stand up for a schedule that makes sense.

There's also something very simple that many big companies could
offer right away that would make a huge difference. It would save
money, attract and retain top talent, and help resolve a national crisis
that affects tens of millions of people every day.

How a Bus Could Solve a
Parenting Crisis

W e lose twenty hours a week," Beth Gaddis says of the
worst time sucker in America. "Ten hours for each of
us." Beth and her husband, Carter, live in a Tampa
suburb—and when we spoke, that's how she described the impact of
commuting on their family life. Her work for a newspaper and his
creating content for corporate websites put them on the road one hour
each way every day. Their employers didn't allow telecommuting.

Public transportation is also lacking. "There was potential there
about three years ago for a high-speed rail, and that could have turned
into commuter rail. The rug got pulled out from under that," Carter
says. "It was very disappointing. I was looking forward to jumping on
a train one day instead of having to sit in my car an hour before and
after work."

Nationwide, the average commute is about twenty-six minutes
each way. But about 8 percent of workers have commutes of an hour
or longer. Nearly six hundred thousand have "megacommutes" of at
least ninety minutes and fifty miles.[1]

Jay Ramsay said his daily commute was thirty-five minutes to
work and, with the congestion at the end of the work day, often two

hours to get home. "Some days I think, 'I just have to find another job,'" he said.

During my years reporting for NPR, I often joked that I was grateful for traffic congestion, which gave the network a huge part of its audience. The truth is I hate traffic. I live just a few miles from work in town, travel in off-hours, and pretty much avoid the congestion. When I look at highways that are clogged daily, I see a failed system. People all over the world deserve better.

If you think of all that time spent in traffic as time that families could be together, you see it in a whole new light. You realize it's a crisis. Our lives are packed enough without this ridiculous waste of time keeping us apart from each other—not to mention making us feel frustrated, stressed, and hurting when we finally get home. "Long commutes cause obesity, neck pain, loneliness, divorce, stress, and insomnia," *Slate* reported.[2]

As we discussed in the last chapter, many companies don't allow telecommuting. But what if there were a way to make everyone happy? Here's a simple proposal: a bus.

Imagine that big companies organize bus pickups for their employees at certain convenient spots in areas where many live. The buses are paid for by the company and used exclusively by its employees. Each bus is equipped with Wi-Fi (that's cheap these days). The moment an employee gets in, sits down, and turns on his or her computer, the workday begins. The worker is on the clock and productive.

The vast majority of white-collar jobs include at least some work that can be done via laptop. With the bus ride as part of their day, workers have already started their productivity by the time they arrive at the office. Near the end of the day, employees board buses back to their cars, working along the way. The bus becomes a mobile office—and time spent working on the bus counts as work hours.

Would employees goof off, fall asleep, and not get work done on the bus? That would be as unlikely as their doing the same at the place of business. On the bus, they'd be surrounded by their colleagues in what the company establishes as a work environment. And companies could easily gauge how much work these employees are getting done on the bus. (Phone calls would not be allowed, so the only sounds on the bus would be people typing or talking quietly with colleagues about work matters.)

All the relevant figures suggest that companies would *save* money by doing this. It would be a leg up on the competition, helping them attract and retain high-quality employees. I asked a lot of dads which they'd choose: a job that paid $5,000 or even $10,000 more than they were getting or a job that had this benefit. Most said they'd choose this one. Also in the company's favor is not having to provide parking for employees who take advantage of this. And there's a good chance that a company could work out some kind of local or state tax break for offering this, because it would pull cars off the road, making the commute faster for drivers. Furthermore, buses can travel in high-occupancy lanes that often move more quickly.

Think this idea can't work? Turns out it already is. Companies in Silicon Valley, like Apple, Genentech, eBay, Yahoo, and Facebook, are among those doing it. "I think it's important," Sheryl Sandberg, COO of Facebook, told me in our interview. "We also have a large number of employees going from location A to location B. So it works for us."

She's right—this exact idea wouldn't work for every major company, though it would work for many big ones. But there are creative solutions that just about any business can come up with. "Technology enables us to be much more flexible employers, and we should be," Sandberg said.

Carter and Jay, whom I mentioned earlier, represent the need to seek creative solutions. Both men have since taken on new jobs, and are much happier. Jay's is closer to home; Carter is working from home. "And I meet the boys off the school bus just about every afternoon," he says.

These kinds of solutions apply best to white-collar workers. For people in service industries and other blue-collar jobs, there's a lot more that needs to be done. They're exemplified by a man in San Francisco whose jungle life changed when he witnessed his father's kidnapping.

In Need of Champions

Marco Ponce grew up in Peru. As a child, he used to play in the jungle with "pocket monkeys" the size of a finger. But his youth ended at nineteen when he witnessed his father's kidnapping. Guerrillas from the Shining Path movement had been intimidating his father, a judge, in his office, shooting at his window, Marco says. "He knew they wanted money and all this stuff, support for them, but he said, 'No, I obey the law.'"

So they seized him on his land, dragged him away, and, Marco says, killed him. "I never see his body. They disappeared him."

The Maoist guerrilla group known for its brutality also took the family's land and all their cattle. The Ponces were left with nothing. There was a more immediate concern, though. The kidnappers had seen Marco. "They believed I was one of the buyers for the cows. They didn't realize I was his son. If they realized, they would maybe kill me. They don't want to have any witnesses."

Marco had to flee Peru right away. He dropped out of school, where he was studying engineering. A combination of buses, planes, and walking across the border from Mexico got him into the United States, where he had relatives. He started working at fast-food joints to get by. But the love of his life was still in Peru. So he snuck back home to get her and brought her to the United States.

Not long after, the two had a son. They didn't know what to do. "It was too hard for us, because it's expensive," he says. So they sent their boy back to Marco's mother in Lima—temporarily, Marco hoped. After a year, when Marco and his wife went back to Peru to see their son, Marco says, "He don't recognize me, his father. I got pain and decide, 'No, I need to take him back. He's my son.'"

Now forty-six and a U.S. citizen, Marco lives with his wife and three children in San Francisco. The language barrier prevented him from ever resuming his engineering education, and he works his fingers to the bone to provide. He holds down three jobs busing tables and tutors some of his kids' friends in math. "I work every day, seven days a week—hours, maybe fourteen, sixteen," he says. His wife works outside the home about five hours a day in addition to caring for the family.

The most heartbreaking part is his lack of contact with his children. "I see them only in the nighttime, when they're sleeping. So, basically, I don't never see my kids."

Marco pulls in $2,500 a month. Of that, $1,500 goes to rent for their two-bedroom apartment. He has thought about moving, but can't afford to lose the rent-controlled home. If the family moved outside San Francisco, it would be too expensive for Marco to travel into the city for work. And the jobs in the other places he's looked don't pay as well.

But Marco has no regrets. "It isn't easy, no. That's why I say I invest—my kids' future. I stay here for my kids to succeed." When his kids grow up, he says, they'll make more money than they would in Peru.

For all the problems facing the "middle class," Marco's story is a reminder that the inability to strike a healthy work-life balance can be even worse for the "working poor." I put these terms in quotes because there are no simple definitions.

There are changes we as a nation can make to fix this, so that all hardworking Americans actually get to see their children. It means addressing the thorny issues of affordable housing, living wages, and paid time off for hourly workers. More than half the working poor, working welfare recipients, and workers who recently left welfare don't have paid leave, and those who do generally have one week or less. Four in ten private-sector workers have no paid sick leave—more than 40 million people, including the vast majority of lower-paid workers.[1]

The debate over food stamps is particularly important to Marco, whose family is just barely priced out of receiving them. "If America gave us food when you need it, for less money, than other people. If I can get from the government help, you know, for milk," Marco says when I ask what would make life better for his family. These issues are hotly debated, and there are legitimate and important concerns about the misuse and abuse of public assistance programs. But no one can argue legitimately that a U.S. citizen should have to work a hundred hours a week to barely get by.

We need to change the dialogue about these issues. They should no longer be framed as battles over taxes, entitlements, or "handouts." It's time to establish a nonpartisan conversation that focuses on a simple question: How can we make sure that hardworking families have the basics? And we must emphasize that "the basics" aren't just food, clothes, and shelter. Parents having time at home with their children is a basic.

Jill Degrafenreed, a hardworking mom of six, just wants a job with benefits—or at least the chance as an hourly employee to be able to accrue parental leave time. "It's so not fair," she says. "I'm a mother first, and then I'm a worker." She'd be willing to accept a payroll tax to help make this possible.

Jill has hourly work in food service, runs a cleaning business with her sister, and, without a college degree, got special training to be a tax preparer. "I've been blessed to have understanding bosses. When my son Kobe was six months old, he was in the hospital for a month. I called my boss and said, 'I don't know when I'll be back.'" That time off was unpaid.

The Center for WorkLife Law is "very involved with trying to get pregnancy accommodations for blue-collar and low-wage women," says director Joan Williams. "I think we can get those through the ADA (Americans with Disabilities Act). I'm also very interested in improving schedules for hourly workers addressing work-life conflict."

Jill experiences that conflict more than most since, in addition to her six children, she helps care for her mother, who has cancer, and her father, who has an unusual illness that left him quadriplegic. Robert, her husband, takes care of his father as well, while scraping by financially. He works as a mechanic and generally holds temp jobs. His income "depends on how much the phone rings," he says.

One thing that would vastly improve their life is affordable health insurance. Jill and Robert are uninsured. Their kids and elderly parents are covered through Medicaid. They're hoping now that "Obamacare" has begun to roll out, there might soon be a good coverage plan they can afford. And they feel that the country in general doesn't do enough to help people on the lower rungs of the economic ladder. "It's a big deal when people start a foundation to feed homeless in Africa and third-world countries, but you have people right here who are hungry," Robert says. "I don't understand why we can't do more for our own people. I know we're trying to be missionaries and help other countries. Why don't we start on the inside and then work out?"

Robert faces another challenge, however, that gets at a tough reality in America. He has a felony on his record for selling drugs to an undercover cop.

He was making good money as a hotel manager until 9/11. The tourism industry was hit especially hard over the next couple of years, and the hotel let him go. "I was job hunting, nothing was coming up, and I still had these kids to feed, so I did what I had to do," he says. He's not proud of it and isn't asking for pity. He's just honest about why he did it. "I wasn't selling on the streets. I was using my phone and met people." For two years, he made "good money." When he got caught, he says, "I didn't do that much time. I went in for seven days. Right at Christmas."

"I was so mad," says Jill. "The day he got locked up we'd been to the Festival of Trees with our sons and at school." Jill knew what Robert was up to and wanted him to stop. "That wasn't the worst thing that could have happened. He could have gotten killed. I always worried about that. It was awful."

Robert says he stopped more than ten years ago. "He hasn't been in any trouble," Jill says. "He hasn't had a speeding ticket since then." But the penalties haven't stopped. Recently, he was working his way up at a company that a temp agency placed him at. "I was promoted two times. I operated two machines and worked in three different divisions. I was doing good." When the company wanted to hire him permanently, paperwork was required—and he acknowledged the felony. The company let him go.

It certainly makes sense that any company would be wary of hiring someone with a felony record. Still, Jill says, "You did the crime, you did the time, you did community service. So how many times are you being punished for the same crime?" They're hoping to get his felony expunged.

There's also a racial element to this, since studies indicate black people, like Robert, are disproportionately arrested and punished for drug crimes. And after getting out of jail, wages among black men grow at a 21 percent slower rate than for white men. Fewer black men ever make it back to the income they had before arrest.[2]

For Robert, there was a happy ending—or at least a happy next step. He and Jill helped people during a snowstorm that paralyzed Atlanta, stranding people on highways all over the city. One man they helped was a truck driver. "If you ever need anything, call me," he told them.

"I need a job," Robert told him. A few months later, the driver's company had an opening. Robert was hired, with full benefits. The application asked only whether he had a criminal record in the previous twelve months.

Although drug-crime legislation is controversial, many of the issues that we as Americans should champion in order to help struggling families aren't controversial at all. A good example is providing resources for children with special needs. Their parents should not be bankrupted.

"I was making $100,000 and now am at the poverty level," says Timothy Welsh, of Catlin, Illinois, who has become known by his Internet name, "Tanner's Dad." Tanner is autistic. Now eighteen, he hasn't spoken since he was four, when his mind regressed to that of a three- to six-month-old baby. "He's my life. I know that. I have no social life," Welsh says. "I live to serve him."

He loves his son deeply, but for Timothy it's an often miserable life. "I've taken the initiative to go to counselors several times, because I've contemplated suicide. I've also contemplated a crime, so I could go to jail and have meals, be warm."

Welsh's wife runs a flower shop, and he has had work on and off in sales over the years. While the public school system is responsible for providing for Tanner until age twenty-two, he requires constant care around the clock. "He doesn't have control of his body," Timothy says. "I sleep by the front door." During the school day, Timothy is busy preparing things for Tanner's care. "When we can afford it, he eats wheat-free and lactose-free. He looks like a ripped supermodel."

Instrumental help can come through community groups and people just offering their assistance, he says. "I boil it down to microbenefits. Pick a family, pick a date. Offer to take over the care for a bit. Something as simple as a movie and a meal can be a respite for a single parent with a special-needs child."

Timothy's experience has changed his mind about the role of society in helping those most in need. "I'm a conservative Christian and I really believe government should be smaller, not bigger. But my eyes have been opened to the needs of the homeless and the poor and the reasons people don't have jobs."

When I asked parents at various income levels about solutions that would help with their financial constraints, one of the most common answers was universal, free pre-K. "It's something this country has to look at," said Adam Cohen, who's raising a son with his wife in Manhattan. "Because at three years old the kid is ready to go to school."

There's heated debate over whether taxpayers should have to cover pre-K for everyone. Most kids that age take part in some kind of program, and opponents of a universal plan argue that a more sensible approach would be a publicly subsidized program for families that can't afford it, such as Head Start.

President Obama wants to provide federal funds to states to help enroll kids from families up to 200 percent of the poverty line. He points to figures suggesting that every dollar spent pays off tremendously in later years by setting kids on the right track.[3] Certainly, some kind of program is needed to make sure that kids from lower-income families don't languish. And offering pre-K would allow some parents to return to the workforce, at least part-time.

My family has benefitted from our access to free pre-K. In Georgia, every child can attend free as long as there's a spot available. These programs are subsidized by the lottery. Our older son loved his program. He's very precocious and a top student. Our second son has just begun pre-K and is enjoying it as well. I'm fortunate to have a good income and wouldn't want anyone who makes less than I do to be without this same option. Tulane professor and MSNBC host Melissa Harris Perry lists universal pre-K as among the most important policies needed for working families, along with universal health care, paid leave for mothers and fathers, raising the minimum wage, and infrastructure improvements to connect workers with "job-rich environments."[4]

When you hear a laundry list of needs, it's natural to wonder whether our society can afford them. The key to understanding all of these is that a country is stronger when children have time with their parents and when parents are able to be a part of the workforce. Children who never get to see their parents often fall into all sorts of troubles, which costs society money. As a nation, we can address these issues and build a stronger, more economically sound society.

For all their struggles, the families I spoke with that are the most strained financially are also happy and hopeful. "We are so close and always there for each other," says Jill Degrafenreed. "We crank the music up and dance!" She's confident that all her kids will find good jobs when they grow up. "That's why we push them."

She calls over Kobe, fourteen, who's getting top grades at school and has decided to become a lawyer. "Like everyone in my family has dealt with the law. Why not have someone on both sides? And I think everything is a competition, and everybody tells me to do better than my father and mother. So I decided why not do better than the whole family."

"Better at what?" I ask.

"Better at life—you won't have to struggle," Jill interjects.

"I don't want to have any regrets," Kobe says. "I just want to do what I can and do the best with my abilities." He'll get that chance because of the hard work Jill and Robert are doing.

Kobe also knows one more thing: he tells me he doesn't want kids. "He's got enough kids in his life," Jill jokes.

Marco, meanwhile, has already had an American dream come true. His son's writing was published in a book that reached President Obama's desk. After the 2008 presidential election, kids around the country wrote to Obama. Marco's son, ten, also named Marco, was among those whose work was published in *Thanks and Have Fun Running the Country: Kids' Letters to President Obama:*

I am writing this letter because I want to stop the war in Iraq and make the economy better. This is important because a lot of people are getting killed shooting at each other. Families are sad and worried about losing their loved ones. Also, the war is very expensive.

Mr. Obama, you should send the troops back to America. We can use the money saved to heal soldiers, and build schools for kids with low incomes, and help families with their needs. Thanks, Mr. Obama, for reading my letter about my problem. I like you being my president. I wish you good luck and to be elected again.[5]

His father tears up with pride as he tells me that he knows the president read the book. He saw a photo in the paper of Obama looking at it. Marco clipped it out and saved it.

It would be safe for Marco to move back to Peru now, where he could live a much more comfortable life. "With $100 a month, I can pay somebody to clean my house, even cook for whole family," he says. Marco's five siblings, all professionals, try to convince him to come back. "They told me they help me to finish school there. They say, 'What are you doing washing dishes over there?' I say, 'Because of my kids. Getting education in America will be more potential, life will be much easier.'"

Everything we've discussed in this section is essential for building a nation centered on valuing families. But some parents believe looking at these issues is putting the cart before the horse. We can't begin to tackle any of these challenges, they say, until we fix the skewed prism through which many Americans view modern parenting. And that, the argument goes, starts with your TV.

PART III

Fixing Pop Culture

The "Doofus Dad" Obsession Must End

Here's how I know modern American dads and moms can rise up together and affect change: we already have. But it wasn't the backward laws, policies, and workplace stigmas that incurred our wrath. It was television.

"We're not the Peter Griffin or the Homer Simpson that we're often portrayed as," blogger Kevin Metzger once told me in an interview for CNN, referring to the stereotypical idiot patriarchs of *Family Guy* and *The Simpsons*.[1] Any time I've interviewed fathers over the years, frustration about portrayals of dads in pop culture has gotten them fired up above all else—particularly what they see in advertisements. Blogger David Holland calls the clueless dad "Madison Avenue's go-to guy."[2]

In 2012, these and many other dads had had enough. The straw that broke the camel's back was a Huggies commercial. "To prove Huggies diapers and wipes can handle anything, we put them to the toughest test imaginable: dads, alone with their babies, in one house, for five days." It showed a mom saying, "Good luck, babe," and dads seeming confused and grossed out. Another Huggies commercial showed dads who didn't change diapers while watching an entire game through "double overtime."

The campaign was obviously offensive. And the fact that a major company was behind it said a lot about our culture. "We need to let go of the notion that it's okay to dis fathers because they're expected to just take it," says Chris Routly, who blogs at DaddyDoctrines.com. He links these portrayals directly to anachronistic policies and stigmas. Society is still telling men that caregiving "is not really their job," he says, linking the problem to my legal battle. "That's why your paternity-leave fight has been so hard. People have a hard time letting go of this idea."

This thinking starts with what we teach children, Chris says. "Boys are not given permission to learn. Girls are handed babies. And when women get pregnant they spend nine months with people trying to prepare them. So they're a little bit ahead." As boys become men, pop culture keeps sending the message that they're somehow naturally less capable of caring for a child, Chris says.

So after the Huggies ads appeared, Chris posted a petition on change.org titled, "We're Dads, Huggies. Not Dummies." He wrote, "These Huggies ads literally use the line, 'Dads push diapers and wipes to the limit.' No, Huggies, dads don't do that. Poor manufacturing does that. A large bottle before naptime does that. Feeding your kid too much fiber does that. Babies do that. But dads don't use diapers and wipes any differently than moms.'"[3]

It got traction in blogs and on social media, and many men and women expressed anger at the company—more than enough to get the attention of Kimberly Clark, Huggies' parent company. On Facebook, the company posted a message from one of its employees, a father (who identified himself only by his first name), saying he was responsible for the ad and meant no offense. "A fact of real life is that dads care for their kids just as much as moms do and in some cases are the only caregivers," he wrote.

More significantly, the company pulled the ads and released a new one offering a very different message. "To prove Huggies wipes can handle anything, we asked real dads to put them to the test with their own babies on spaghetti night," the ad said, showing a group of men cooking for their babies and feeding them.

And the company went a step farther. "Huggies sent its brand manager and his team to the Dad 2.0 Summit, basically on bended knee, to say, 'Tell us the story here,'" says summit cofounder John Pacini. "That conversation was covered by *Ad Age, Adweek,* a lot of the trade publications."

It was also covered by me, on CNN.com and HLN. "Being a dad, I just love this story, and thankfully some dads took action," my colleague Mike Galanos said, setting up our conversation on air. "What do they want for Father's Day? For the media to stop portraying dads as buffoons. Doofus dads, right? I mean, that's all we ever see. It's not just one show; it's practically every show."

All this attention made clear to TV writers and ad makers that if they grab at the idiot dad trope, they'll be in for a headache. But Huggies' experience also showed that if a company does right by fathers, it will win support. The NYC Dads Group ended up praising Huggies publicly for "raising the bar for dads in advertising."[4]

"So now the industry is listening," says Pacini. Companies that are listening are profiting. At the forefront is Unilever, which in recent years has launched a series of products through its "Dove Men+Care" brand.

"There was a marketing opportunity from an emotional standpoint, a huge gap in the market," says Unilever vice president Rob Candelino. "Nobody was celebrating real dads. There were the quintessential archetypes of dad as buffoon or dad as alpha male. But nobody was talking about dads as real men."

Unilever had already seen that talking to "real women" works. Its "Campaign for Real Beauty" used no models or airbrushing. So during the 2010 Super Bowl, Dove launched a new campaign with a commercial called "Manthem." It showed a boy growing up to become a father. The narrator asked, "Now that you're comfortable with who you are, isn't it time for comfortable skin?"

"We did a lot of research—an exhaustive amount," Candelino says. "Virtually every man we talked to said, 'I'm going on this journey. Sometime in my mid to late thirties, I reached a point where I'm figuratively comfortable in my own skin. I've realized I'm not going to be an astronaut, I'm not going to be a pro baller—but I'm okay with that.'

"The single most transformational event in a man's life is fatherhood, the birth of a child, and the child rearing that happens. Nothing moves a man like that. That is a sweet spot. If we want to celebrate the poignant moments in a man's life, then fatherhood is rich territory. Guys are emotionally vulnerable, open, reassessing everything in their life. So insert a brand that gets it, showcases that, talks to guys in a way that is respectable, respectful, and says, 'Hey, we're here with you.'" The campaign brought "wonderful out-of-the-gate sales, fantastic success," Candelino says. "As a brand it's grown every year, and we continue to be happy about the results."

Over the following years, Dove took that messaging further. During Super Bowl 2015, it launched the "Real Strength" campaign to "celebrate the caring character of today's men, recognizing how care makes them stronger." The ad focused on dads having beautiful, heartfelt moments with their kids. It celebrated "men who embrace their caring side, which is no longer antithetical to being strong, but is instead the hallmark of modern, well-rounded masculinity," the company said.

"The core of male masculinity today is rooted in his strength of character," said Dr. Michael Kimmel, who studies and writes about masculinity and advised Dove on the campaign. "Traits like integrity, authenticity, and how he cares for himself and those around him are integral to how a man perceives his own masculinity today—versus physical strength, power, and affluence that prior generations may have prioritized."

Unilever also released a survey of men in the U.S., UK, Germany, Brazil, and China. It found that 86 percent of men say masculinity has changed from their father's generation, but only 7 percent of men say they can relate to the way the media depicts masculinity. Nine out of ten men see their caring side as a sign of strength.[5] These numbers are for men who chose to take part in the survey, and it's quite possible some Neanderthal types would opt not to. Still, the figures are telling.

Other companies are seeing the light as well. Toyota also won plaudits (including from me) for an ad celebrating dads during Super Bowl 2015. In fact, many of the headlines took note of this new phenomenon. Two from my colleagues at CNN included "Dad gets a makeover in Super Bowl ads" and "The ads that made this dad cry." "It's the Dadvertising that really got us," *The Huffington Post* wrote.

The lesson is that modern dads have economic power. If we want more companies to stop insulting us as a group, we have to harness that power. There's some dispute over just how much "purchasing power" dads have or are exerting. One study found more than half of dads say they're the primary grocery shoppers,[6] while another found that moms are still the primary shoppers in 80 percent of families.[7] Still, dads are growing in this role, and companies have clear economic incentive to appeal to them.

The trend is going in the right direction. Blogger Zach Rosenberg, who had railed against depictions of fathers, did an extensive examination to see how things are changing.[8] He studied 140 commercials and rated 94 as good or mostly good and 18 as bad. The rest were neutral.

This isn't to say the battle is over. It remains an important fight. "There's still a fair amount of judgment and humor about the bumbling dad," says dad and former Parents.com executive editor Michael Kress.

I took on Clorox for an offensive web post in 2013. "Saying 'No-no' is not just for baby. Like dogs or other house pets, new dads are filled with good intentions, but lacking the judgment and fine motor skills to execute well," the post read. It also said a new dad will take his child for a walk in a cold, rain-soaked stroller and only after ten minutes begin to wonder, "Why is this baby crying so much?" At that point, he'll notice his child is wearing "a short-sleeved summer onesie."

Weirdly, the post also said that some new dads "have been inspired by raunchy comedies to bring babies to inappropriate places like casinos, pool halls, and poetry readings." Yes, poetry readings. It made me wonder if whoever wrote this was sniffing a little too much Clorox. When I wrote about this in a CNN.com column, the company sent me a statement saying it was attempted humor, a "light-hearted comparison between bachelor lives and new-parent lives."[9] Later, the company tried to claim it was actually an effort to "poke fun at the caricature of 'the hapless dad.'" Either way, Clorox got the message. It pulled the post.

Of course, some of the comment-section riffraff responded to my column by saying dads should stop being so sensitive. Every time a dad speaks up against these portrayals, we get those kinds of remarks, and often much worse. "I got hate mail from men trying to belittle my masculinity, saying I make 'manly men' physically ill," says Chris Routly. "What it really showed me is a lot of people have a vested interest in keeping these strict roles in place." Just as biased depictions of any group should not be tolerated, Chris says, "We can't brush these things away."

Charlie Capen, a Hollywood actor you've probably seen on TV, is working stealthily from the inside to try to end these stereotypes. "I just started going in for dad roles, which is weird. I guess I now have enough gray hairs," he says. "I get called in for commercials and see the script with the dumb dad, and I'm like, 'I'm not going to play it that way,'" he says in a sing-songy voice. "I just subvert it."

So far he hasn't gotten these dad roles. "My friends who don't have kids got those parts," he says, "but I have influenced friends who are commercial copywriters. Brands are even more sensitive now, because women don't want to see men picked on so much. The team aspect is there." He's right. Moms speak out about these kinds of ads as profusely as dads do. Every time there's another offensive ad or web post, I hear about it from both women and men—and not just those with children.

There may have been a time when this kind of skewering was much more harmless. A study of comics found images of "incompetent" fathers dating back to the 1940s.[10] Meanwhile, on TV, most images of dads were idealized, from 1950s shows like *Leave It to Beaver* to the 1970s *The Brady Bunch* and 1980s *The Cosby Show*. By the late 1980s, shows wanted to distance themselves "from the corny, syrupy stuff," Bob Thompson, director of the Bleier Center for Television and Popular Culture at Syracuse University, told me for a CNN .com column. Along came *Married with Children* and *The Simpsons*.

"Comedy is about inversion—taking people who are in authority and control and making them the butt of jokes," Thompson said. In a society "that has been so dominated by men . . . comedy is naturally going to play against that."[11]

But context changes everything. Now, parents are ready to rise up against our rigid, outdated structures. That requires opening up the minds of those who produce pop-culture portrayals. Fortunately, we have a powerful leader—a man proving that if you build shows around three-dimensional, believable parents of both genders, viewers will come.

The Man Who's Changing Television

J ason Katims did the seemingly impossible. He took a show about perhaps the most traditionally macho American institution, football, and turned it into a show about a modern American dad. Then he turned that show, *Friday Night Lights,* into the story of a man who gives up his work dreams so that his wife can achieve hers. And Katims did this in such an impassioned, riveting way that he took millions along for the ride.

But he was just starting. Next, he brought TV parents into the new millennium as showrunner of *Parenthood,* the drama that opened eyes, hearts, and minds through pop culture's deepest, most three-dimensional portraits. Katims decided to make one central character a stay-at-home dad who gave up work as a contractor building houses to be home with his family. He's every bit as "manly" as the other guys. With nuance and respect, Katims set about tracing the struggles of family patriarch Zeek Braverman in grappling with how his sons parent and what it says about their, and his, manliness.

I spoke with Katims about how he has infused his own experience as a modern dad into the TV landscape.

LEVS: When you began writing shows, did you make a conscious effort to portray fathers in a three-dimensional way?

KATIMS: I didn't set out to change the way people think about anything. But it's rewarding when you get that kind of feedback from what you're putting out there. With the writers and actors, I always try to come back to the question: What would really happen? What would these characters really do? I try to have all of us think of that as our responsibility. Obviously in television, fictional entertainment, we're jamming a lot into a short time, so we take license. But we try to take those moments, dig in, and make them as real as possible.

LEVS: *Friday Night Lights* was based on a movie, but you designed it your own way. How did people respond early on to the central character?

KATIMS: We got a tremendous amount of feedback—this kind of real love for Taylor as a dad, husband, and coach. I had never thought of doing it as a show about football. It was the story of a small town and a family. And the coach was a father, obviously to his children, but by extension also to everyone on that football team. The beauty of that show was the surrogate parenting story.

LEVS: Did you get any complaints about his character?

KATIMS: No, people loved him. Some complained about his stubbornness, particularly in the last season, when his wife, Tami, had the opportunity to move. It was hard for him to make the decision based on her and not him. To me it felt very real, cutting to something very deep. At the end of the day, roles are changing. But who's following whom? On the show, Tami had important work and arguably was his boss. But it always felt like his coaching the team took precedence over everything in their lives. It was very much a story about a traditional family unit because, more than others, coaches move from town to town. Basically this family's life was moving to several different towns, always led by him. For him to actually be faced with this decision was tough. I think some of our viewers were frustrated with his stubbornness. We didn't get any complaints from people saying it was wrong to ultimately move.

LEVS: With *Parenthood,* you made the choice to have a stay-at-home dad, but not in a "Mr. Mom" way. It wasn't supposed to be funny. Did anyone say, "This won't sell?"

KATIMS: No, people were supportive. I was working with Ron Howard and Brian Grazer. They wanted it to feel real, something relevant to today. They were on board. I think they did envision a more comedic show. But it wound up really finding its voice over the course of the first season.

LEVS: You said the story lines reflect your experience. You grew up without a lot of discussing of emotions among men.

KATIMS: Yes. I grew up in Brooklyn, the youngest of three kids. I don't remember my dad saying "I love you" or hugging me. Not that I thought my father was unavailable—it was just the norm. But when I became a father, I consciously wanted to be more expressive to my kids of those feelings.

LEVS: I tell my kids I love them constantly.

KATIMS: It's like we're overdoing it!

LEVS: Where do you think that comes from?

KATIMS: In me, it's an unsung yearning for a more open communication with my parents. And it's just more who my wife and I are. I was raised by parents who had gone through tough times. My father's parents split up, which was very rare. He was the son of a single parent who had been through the Great Depression. I think there was something in that World War II male mentality of "You have to be strong. Suck it up. Don't cry. No crying in baseball." Those types of things. That was how I was raised, but it's not who I am or turned into as a person.

LEVS: In this new era, do you think TV will follow your lead and start to represent more "real" dads?

KATIMS: There aren't a lot of shows that focus on parenting. I'd love to see more. Right now that's not what the networks are looking to do, which is sad to me. These shows are important, because ultimately what's most meaningful in life is family. But where there are dads on TV, I do think things are looking better. There are more sensitive portrayals of people in general, and I think the audience is demanding that. They have seen great TV where people are so real and so challenging. That sets a higher bar for us. We have to step up to that.

Although dads like Jason can do a lot of good, there's also another, more dangerous stereotype of fatherhood. To eradicate this one, we need both entertainment and news media to join forces.

Media and the Fear of Men

I t's far worse than the image of the hapless buffoon. It damages families, skews the minds of young children, isolates fathers raising kids alone, and even prevents some kids from having male role models at all. It's the idea that men are dangerous and only women should be trusted.

"Yes, there are shit bombs like Jerry Sandusky," says Don Jackson, the loving father whose former top-secret government work involved keeping Americans safe. "But there are hundreds of thousands of guys who are the opposite. You have to have the healthy fear, but don't let it rule your thinking."

Rick Martin, my colleague and a brilliant TV manager, thinks the news is partly to blame. "We hear about these men. Or fathers who kill their families and then themselves. We hear so many negative stories," he says.

"We need to start presenting a culture of success. There's so much negativity. Somehow as a culture we have to create positivity celebrating men who are successful as fathers. Through series, news programs, magazines, newspapers, we need to be showing role models." Rick wants a male version of *Oprah*—a show that will celebrate great things men, and specifically dads, are doing.

In the years since I started covering fatherhood on mainstream TV and online, some news organizations have come a long way, presenting more stories about good dads. Still, there aren't enough. Default thinking for general news segments about parenting is still often to focus largely on moms. When dads are interviewed, it's often presented as a special report focusing on men—rather than a general guide or sound bite from a parent who just happens to be male. And this sexism again plagues both genders. When women executives are interviewed, they're sometimes asked about work-life balance, while male executives aren't. (Good rule of thumb for fellow journalists: either ask both genders or neither.)

Rick says more talk of fatherhood in the news will help open minds. "As an analogy, it's like with black people like me. You know, a lot of people, when they saw a black person, they'd think, 'Oh, let me clutch my purse.' It took a culture of understanding that, you know, hey, not everybody who looks like that is going to come rob you. And I think society needs to create that culture of success that helps people understand, 'Hey, it's okay seeing a dad walk down the street with his two kids and everyone's having a good time.'"

Sadly, that actually is something far too many people need to learn. "There's an underlying sense of fear of men in society," says Whit Honea, a dad, blogger, and writer in the LA area. "A dad will be out with his kid, the kid is upset, and a woman will come up and ask the kid if he or she is okay. They'll think the worst. They don't see a father with a child. They see a kidnapper. You'd never hear of a woman with a crying child in public and someone assuming the worst immediately."

To some dads, this fear was epitomized by a moment on the daytime TV talk show *Bethenny,* when three stay-at-home fathers were being interviewed. "When it comes to play groups, I don't know how comfortable I'd feel dropping my daughter off with just the male being home—there's no wife home, and I'm dropping my daughter off. I personally just don't feel comfortable," one woman told them. She seemed well meaning, and added, "I know that women can also be child molesters and pedophiles."

One of the panelists interrupted her. "Wait, wait, wait. Stop, stop, stop," said stay-at-home dad and blogger Doyin Richards. "You're saying you don't feel comfortable leaving your kids with a man? That's more of a you problem than a man problem, right?" The audience applauded.

But to her credit, the woman who admitted her discomfort was only vocalizing what many people believe. She went on to cite images she sees on TV, including in fictional shows often "based on" true events, like *Law and Order.*

"We need to have more reality out there about parenting and what fatherhood really is," says Lance Somerfeld, who was one of the three dads on the show. "We need more TV shows and more news segments demonstrating the realities of fatherhood rather than what the perception is."

National statistics show that women carry out more acts of child abuse, both through negligence and of the kind that leads to death.[1] That's important to keep in mind when making default assumptions about gender, but it's also important to understand in context. Women spend more time with children, so it would only make sense that most abuse, which is usually in the form of neglect, would be carried out by women. Men commit most of the sexual abuse.[2] Men are the vast majority of predators. (Though it's important to note that some of the misguided assumptions about gender that we've discussed in this book make it especially difficult to detect and prosecute female perpetrators.)[3] Some local studies have found that more cases of violent abuse involved male perpetrators.[4] Still, it's important to understand that a mom is not automatically safer than a dad. As parents, we have a responsibility to get to know whoever is watching over our children.

Many dads complain that we teach kids to fear men from a very early age, imprinting them with gender bias. And on this point, they're right. Even my family is guilty. We originally taught our kids what "safety experts" had told us to teach them: if you're ever lost, find a "mom with kids" and ask for help. If you can't, then find someone in uniform.

"The unspoken corollary being: 'Because a *man* might drag you off and dye your hair in the bathroom and smuggle you out and rape you,'" outspoken mom Lenore Skenazy wrote in a blog post.[5] "What is the message we're giving our kids? 'Any man could possibly be a perv.' And as that message ricochets through pop culture right back to us, we too have started to distrust any male who has anything to do with a child."

Whit Honea was seated with a group of dads at the Mom 2.0 Conference when a woman came and joined them. As Whit tells it, "She owns a popular line of videos for kids. Within two minutes she's telling us her company's philosophy instructing kids that if they're lost, find a mommy. 'So if a child is lost in a park, you want them to walk by three obvious dads with kids to find a mommy?' I asked. She listed things: men are violent, men commit these crimes. We all looked at her, like, in disbelief."

As parents we want to keep our kids safe. But as just about all adults know, the only adults at playgrounds are there with kids they're responsible for. Anyone should be wary of an adult, or even a teenager, who isn't there with a child. If my kids need help, they now know it's okay to go up to any parent whose kids seem comfortable with him or her.

"I totally agree with you," says Nancy McBride, executive director at the National Center for Missing and Exploited Children. Giving this gender neutral advice is fine, she says.

Nancy says in public speeches she used to tell a joke: If a child approaches a mother, she'll try to reunite him with his parents right away—because she certainly doesn't want another child to have to watch over. "It always gets a good laugh," she says.

The gender-specific recommendation that kids ask a nearby mom for help also used to be in the center's publications, "but four or five years ago we took it out," she says.

"My position is that it's up to the parent or guardian. The important thing is to identify what we call low-risk helping adults, so children don't feel surrounded by a sea of strangers and there's nobody they can go to for help. The mom was never the first choice. The first choice is always the police officer, or the sales clerk with the name badge, or somebody in a position of authority who hopefully has been trained at least a little as to what to do. Many store associates have at least some training."

But even without teaching kids the "find a mommy" rule, many people nevertheless communicate fear of men to children in a subtler way, through social rejection.

Chris Bernholdt is one of the nicest guys you could meet. Six foot seven and bald, with a huge, bright smile, he gushes about his three kids. He tears up with joy when recounting how his amazing dad, wearing long underwear, danced around the house with all four of his sons. Chris is an art teacher turned stay-at-home father in Philadelphia. A gentle, lovable guy.

When he took his first child to a playground, he saw a group of moms and walked over to introduce himself. "They turned away and closed off their circle," he says. "They were concerned about this strange man, even though I was there with my son." Chris soon found out that other dads were having the same experience. So he created the Philly Dads Group, which now has more than 150 members. "We can socialize and talk about being a dad when things get rough and you don't know where to turn."

Other dad groups across the country have the same backstory. Chris Routly was a stay-at-home dad near Allentown, Pennsylvania, who sought out camaraderie and play dates for his kid. He asked whether he could join a moms' group. "When I presented it to the other members of the group, I was really surprised by the feedback," says Jenae Holtzhafer, who was the organizer. The group rejected him.

Some of the reasons are understandable. Some women didn't want to breastfeed with a man around or just wanted bonding time with other women. Some also said they were afraid of what would happen if they held an event at home and he was the only other parent to show up. I asked Jenae whether some of the women felt uncomfortable with or even fearful of a stay-at-home dad. "I think that was one of the concerns," she said. "There were several other men who had also applied." Of the group's thirty members, Jenae says, she was the only one who wanted to say yes.

Facebook executive Tom Stocky experienced this circumspection during his paternity leave. "I didn't like being the only dad at the playground, getting cautiously eyed as moms pulled their kids a bit closer. It probably didn't help that I tried to lighten the mood the first time by saying, 'Don't worry, I'm not going to nab your kid. I already got this one.' I felt awkward at the mid-day baby music class, like I was impinging on an established mom circle, so I switched to the 5:00 P.M. one that had more dads."[6]

For women to "lean in" more at work, men need to be welcomed into the world of stay-at-home parenthood. Sheryl Sandberg says she always reaches out to dads on the playground. "You have to play with the dad. It's really important."

Some men believe it would also help combat one of the greatest social ills in America: the number of kids who don't have fathers at all. Don Jackson says single moms could strike up friendships with great dads who might become wonderful role models for their kids, but fear is holding them back. "If you're a guy, what's the incentive to go up to a complete stranger and help? Why would you if you're being judged?"

He acknowledges that it makes sense for moms to have a healthy sense of protection, making sure nobody's going to harm their child. "But at the same time, not everybody's a threat. My thinking is, I'm human, you're human; let's share our parenting ideas and experiences."

In drawing this link, Don shines a light on a reality that's been in the shadows: the same forces holding back women at work and men at home are also exacerbating the fatherlessness crisis. We can't fix one while ignoring the other.

PART IV

Fatherlessness

The Truth About Fatherlessness

I t's the central irony of modern parenthood and one of the biggest problems our nation faces. Although it's true that never before have so many dads been so involved in their kids' lives, never before have so many children been without their fathers.

Fatherlessness gets a lot of attention. But here's what doesn't: the fact that the problem is deeply entwined with the other issues we've looked at in this book. The different expectations placed on women and men, the stigmas that hurt us all, and the exhaustive schedules of today's parents contribute to the crisis of absent dads. Fatherhood activists also rightfully point out that there's a danger in the way the country is responding to fatherlessness. If we keep going down this road, we'll make these problems worse. The flip side of that is the good news: the things we need, like better policies and an end to stigmas, will help get more dads involved in their kids' lives.

But before we delve into this, it's time for a badly needed reality check. Talk of fatherlessness in America is filled with inaccuracies and misleading statistics. It's another example of how misunderstood and mischaracterized figures generate false headlines.

Some articles and websites say one-third of U.S. children, or even more than 40 percent, live in homes without their fathers. Some say it's about 24 million kids. These numbers are inflated. For starters, these are often based on assessments of how many kids live without their biological fathers, so they're including kids with adoptive dads and stepfathers who are dads to them in every way except by blood. But even if you use this broad definition, the current numbers still aren't that high.

Another figure you see often is that 17 million kids—nearly a quarter of the kids in America—are fatherless. Again, this is inflated. Fortunately, we don't have this many fatherless children. Census figures show that 17 million kids live in homes with just one parent, their mother. That's about 24 percent of kids, up from 21 percent in 1991.[1] The biggest reason is the increase in couples who never married. Many of those couples break up, even if they planned to stay together when the kids were born.[2] The rise in births to unmarried U.S. women peaked in 2008, but the number remains high—about 4 in 10 births, according to federal statistics.[3]

But many of these kids are not "fatherless." The homes that they are registered as living in, sometimes for school purposes, are with their mothers. But some of these kids still spend time with their fathers every week. One in six dads who live apart from their kids still talk with them about their day every day. About a third don't talk with their kids at all. One in four bathe and dress their kids several times a week or every day. But most of the others never do.[4]

This is why the terms "single mother" and "single father" can be misleading. The person might be both single and a parent, but not parenting alone. "My dad hates when my mom calls herself a single mom," a friend told me. "People assume he's not in my life, but he's as much in my life as my mom is."

"Fatherlessness" can mean different things to different people, so there's no way to say how many American kids are experiencing it. Many of these kids who do spend some time with their dads need more of it. By emphasizing real numbers I'm not for a second suggesting that this isn't a crisis. It absolutely is.

There are cases of involuntary absence—for example, dads who are denied access to their kids. But most absentee dads could be in their children's lives if they made the effort. One child whose father ignores him or her is one too many. The fact that the figure is in the millions is disgusting. Men who shirk their fatherhood responsibilities infuriate good fathers everywhere.

"This guy sucks. He gives us all a bad name," one man I interviewed said of the father he replaced. His stepson, whom he's raising as his own, went through a serious illness, and the boy's father fled. "He decided to leave, said, 'I can't handle this.' He went off cavorting with a young woman." The man is now "a dad in theory," who gets his son each summer, but "still goes to parties and goes out a lot at night. He gets a babysitter."

Some absentee dads have new families and are active, involved fathers to the children they live with. That's the case with a friend of mine who now lives in Bermuda with his beautiful wife and children. He's a fantastic dad to them, but never sees his daughter from a previous marriage that ended badly, even though he could. She lives far away. "It kills me today and will always weigh heavily on my heart," he says.

Numerous studies show that kids who don't have their fathers are more likely to suffer a long list of problems. "There is a 'father factor' in nearly all of the societal issues facing America today," the National Fatherhood Initiative says.[5] Kids without dads are more likely to live in poverty, struggle with behavioral problems, commit crimes, turn to drugs, become parents at a young age, and do all sorts of other things we don't want our kids to do.

These families are often "emotionally and spiritually impoverished because dad's missing," says Jim Daly, president and CEO of Focus on the Family. Getting absentee fathers back in the picture would be like a "silver bullet" for our culture, he believes. "I'm glad President Obama is talking about this. What we need are dads committed to their families."

Some dads give up because they feel they aren't good enough.

"The reason I walked away is because, at the moment, I wasn't the man that I wanted to be for [my kids]," a father named Dwayne remarked on *Oprah's Lifeclass*. "I wasn't worthy to be in their life because I wasn't the man that I would want for them."[6]

One of the biggest reasons dads feel inadequate is that they still believe fatherhood means providing financially. So the same problem fueling backward policies and stigmas is also warping men's sense of what it means to be a good dad.

"We need to educate the culture," says Vince DiCaro, who spent years as vice president of the National Fatherhood Initiative. "We need a dialogue showing that everyone needs a good dad—a guy who's dedicated, involved, responsible. And we have to make sure that moms understand that dads are important, because often moms are the gatekeepers."

He and many other fatherhood activists worry that things are getting worse because Americans are being sent a message that fathers are irrelevant—or, at least, much less important as parents than moms are. "Did you see this ridiculous article?" Vince wrote me one day, up in arms over an article in *Slate*. Entitled "Just Say No," it stated that "for white working-class women, it makes sense to stay single mothers" and not have the children's fathers be involved in their lives.[7] "This is completely absurd and is what is actually leading to deeper inequality in our nation and damaging children's life prospects," Vince complained.

The article argued that for financial reasons, involving a father who might not have steady work can be damaging to the mother: "Although it defies logic, socioeconomic, cultural, and economic changes have brought white working-class women . . . to the point where going it alone can be the wiser choice."[8]

As a financial study of marriage, the article was interesting and made some solid points. Marrying means assuming your partner's debts, and if your partner is unreliable or unable to hold a steady job, there are financial incentives to remain single. What horrified Vince about the article is that it equated lack of marriage with keeping the child's father out altogether. It didn't question the ethics of that choice.

The piece focused on a mother named Lily. She has "let" the father, Carl, see the child, but "he hasn't pressed for more involvement, and Lily is happy to keep it that way. If Carl wants more contact, he would have to take a series of legal steps, including filing a court case, paying the several hundred dollars it would cost for paternity testing, obtaining a court order, and enforcing it if Lily doesn't cooperate voluntarily."

Why would anyone be okay with this? Fathers should be encouraged to be in their kids' lives for the sake of the children. Sadly, there is an increasing tendency in our society to see single mothering as good or neutral. More Americans have come to believe that a fatherless home is not a problem. That includes 13 percent of the country, up from 8 percent in 2007. The numbers are more striking among young people. Only 42 percent of adults under thirty think single motherhood is "a big problem" in America,[9] while large majorities of older parents do.

I have friends who are wonderful mothers doing it on their own. Another friend chose a donor from a sperm bank and is getting set to have a child on her own. "I've tried finding the right guy, and it's just not happening for me," she said. I know she'll be a great mom, and I support her wholeheartedly. She also has relatives, including her own father and brother, nearby who have offered to help.

President Obama grew up the child of a single mom, who had him when she was a teenager. President Clinton also grew up the son of a single mom. We can all celebrate these and other hardworking, committed women who took on the burden of single parenting with tremendous love and success. The key is to do so without denigrating the role of the father or contributing to the misperception that dads aren't necessary.

This is also why some dads I interviewed said they're careful in how they express support for the growing number of same-sex couples having kids. "It's a third rail, I warn you. I've brought this up and been told, 'You're intolerant, you're hateful.'" says Paul Banas, publisher of *Pregnancy Magazine*. "It's a huge issue."

Paul supports gay couples having adoption rights, but he doesn't want the growing support for same-sex parents to drown out the importance of having close role models of each gender. "Someone like me, growing up without a dad—when you lived that, you know it's a big thing," Paul says. "My parents were separated when I was two and divorced when I was five. My father moved across country. He called me every two weeks on the phone. We chatted, and I saw him twice a year."

Paul and many other dads who are active in speaking out about the importance of fathers "are trying to fill a hole that they want to see filled for other kids, because they know what it's like to be without a father," he said. So in conversations with same-sex parents, he's glad to see when they "go out of their way" to find a surrogate that fits that male or female role, because they instinctively feel it's important to have both sexes. Of course, some moms take on roles or have parenting styles similar to what a lot of dads have, and vice versa.

In interviews with two-dad couples for this book, I asked about this. "It's our mothers, our sisters," said Brian Stephens, who is raising a son, Clark, with his partner Andy Miller in Austin. "My mom lives in town, and Clark stays with her sometimes," Andy said. "She picks him up at school two or three days a week. And Brian's family is not far away in Dallas."

I told them there have been a few times that I've seen what one of my boys was going through and said to my wife, "I think this is a dad thing. Let me talk to him." That's not an option when both parents are dads. So, I asked, does that ever cause friction?

"I'm used to being 'the mom,' and I don't usually say that term," Brian said. "My style, when you actually step back and look at my life, is more maternal than paternal as we stereotypically think of those things." Of course, the fact that Brian is a dad makes his actions every bit as "paternal" as Andy's. But the two men told me they find that when they disagree over how to handle a situation, it's often similar to the way a heterosexual couple might disagree, and they just work it out.

Although making sure kids in two-dad households have female role models is important to Andy and Brian, it doesn't worry them or many other dads as much as the converse does—making sure that kids in two-mom households have male role models. That's partly because kids are generally surrounded by women—caregivers, teachers, their moms' friends, their friends' moms—and also because no one's worried that American moms are in danger of being seen as irrelevant.

I asked Idit Klein about this. She and her wife are talking about having kids of their own. "I think about having many nourishing people who love my kids in their lives who can reflect many different aspects of ways of being in the world. Because none of us knows if we have a boy, if we have a girl, what kind of boy, what kind of girl they're going to be. Not every boy remains a boy, not every girl remains a girl. I have no desire to raise anyone in a single-sex atmosphere."

It would also benefit society to get more male role models into schools. Chris Bernholdt was one of two men teaching at a big public school just outside Chicago that included kindergarten all the way through eighth grade. He taught art; the other guy taught gym. That's not unusual. Only 2 percent of pre-K and kindergarten teachers nationwide are men. The number goes up to 18 percent for elementary and middle school.[10] A Stanford study found that boys do better with male teachers, and the growing gap in schools, with boys falling behind girls, could be helped if there were more male teachers.[11]

Chris's school hired one more male teacher while he was there. "There was one guy who wanted to be a kindergarten teacher, and he got the job. He was a big guy, six foot nine, a teddy bear. It was critical for us to show these kids, who didn't have any men to give them encouragement, that they could be the best they could be. Many of these kids weren't used to seeing positive male role models."

The school was 90 percent African American, Chris says. That brings us to perhaps the most misunderstood part of the fatherlessness crisis. Despite the stereotypes, black dads are in some ways the *most* active and involved in their kids' lives.

How Black Dads Are Doing
Best of All

(But There's Still a Crisis)

Robert Bell has seven children. The thirty-seven-year-old got an early start. His first daughter was born when he was seventeen. "No more fun, time to take care of some babies," he says, looking back at what it was like. "I was 100 percent dad ever since. With the rest it was just smooth sailing."

He and his high-school girlfriend broke up, but raised their daughter together. It never occurred to him to walk away. "Because my dad did," he says. "There isn't anything worse than waking up on your birthday or any day without your daddy. He isn't calling or checking on you. So I wasn't going to do that. I saw people running away on their kids. When I made my baby, after I saw her for the first time, there was no way I was going to let someone else raise her."

Robert had his next six kids with Jill Degrafenreed, and the two eventually married. They live in Stone Mountain, Georgia. Jill says Rob's commitment as a father is one of the things that attracted her to him. Her dad was like his. "My father was on drugs and stayed away. My mom and dad split when I was thirteen, and he just figured rather than be around and on drugs, he'd rather stay away. I really never got a chance."

It's the opposite in their household. As I interview Rob and Jill, four of their kids jump around, dancing to music. The younger ones take breaks to come crawl all over Rob. "My kids all love me to death," he says with a contented smile.

Rob is black. Given how widespread the stereotype of the absentee black father is, you might think he's an exception. He isn't. Most black fathers live with their children and take good care of them. In fact, on average, they're even more hands-on than other dads. "If you look at the data for co-residential black fathers, they're more heavily involved in activities than white or Hispanic fathers," says researcher Jo Jones.

The data she refers to are in a report called "Fathers' Involvement with Their Children," the seminal study she coauthored for the Centers for Disease Control and Prevention (CDC). It found that among men who live with their children, "black fathers (70 percent) were most likely to have bathed, dressed, diapered, or helped their children use the toilet every day compared with white (60 percent)." Among dads who don't live with their children, black fathers also had a slightly better track record than white ones. One-third of "non-coresidential" black fathers did not do any of those activities with their kids, compared to 39 percent of white fathers.[1] If you look at these figures more broadly and ask how many dads take care of their kids every day or several times a week, you see things are just about even between black and white dads, Jones points out.

There are ways that black dads fared worse in the study. For example, more don't read to their kids. But that's the point: the reality of black fatherhood is much more mixed than the stereotype suggests. The CDC report marked "the debunking of the black-fathers-being-absent myth," Jones says.

She's right, but only in the sense that *most* black dads are not absent. There is still very bad news: the fatherlessness crisis is worse in the African American community. This is another case in which you have to get past the headlines and into the real numbers to understand what's going on.

Most black dads live with their kids—but "most" only means more than half. The percentage of black dads who live apart from their kids is larger than it is for any other racial group. There are about 2.5 million black fathers living with their children, and about 1.7 million living apart from them.[2] And while many of those 1.7 million still see their children, many others don't. In short, the percentage of dads who don't see their kids is bigger in the African American community than it is for other racial groups.

It gets worse. Government studies have found that most black children don't live with their fathers.[3] This seems confusing, right? Most black dads live with their kids, but most black kids don't live with their dads. How can this be?

It's actually simple. Imagine that I tell you about two families. In one, the dad is active and involved. He has three kids. In the other, the dad is completely absent. That family has five kids. I can tell you that half the dads are involved or that most of the kids are fatherless.

The CDC study I mentioned counted black *fathers.* When studies have instead counted black *children,* they found that only one in three lives with two married parents, compared to three quarters of white kids. Half of black kids live in single-mother homes.[4] This is the figure President Obama cited when he said, "If you're African American, there's about a one-in-two chance you'll grow up without a father in your house."[5] But it's actually, tragically, even more than that. Some kids, for example, don't live with their moms or dads. They live with grandparents, other relatives, or elsewhere. So the number living without their fathers is actually a little over half. And although many of these kids do have their dads in their lives, as with any other race, many don't.

Part of the problem is what I call "serial impregnators"—absent dads of any race who go around having a lot of babies. Given how all these numbers shake out, as a percentage of the population, this absentee father crisis is particularly acute for black children.

For an NPR story, I visited a public housing project. Due to Atlanta demographics, virtually all the residents of that specific project were black. I had all the interviews I needed within an hour, but decided to spend hours more knocking on doors to get to know families and hear their stories. I knocked on every door. About two dozen were answered. In every case, it was a single woman with multiple children. About half were pregnant.

"It's a matter of self-worth. It's a matter of education," says Roland Martin, nationally syndicated columnist and pundit who hosts a radio show on NewsOne, which focuses on the African American community. "I guarantee you with many of those folks, we can go back and look at where they stand educationally, where they stand in terms of literacy. They are also trapped in a cycle. That's the key. You have to deal with their self-worth. A lot of these folks who are having babies want somebody to love, because they themselves never were loved."

That's what some young women told me when I was on a reporting trip to some of the poorest areas of Mississippi. They said they wanted babies, so someone would love them. (None of these issues is in any way limited to the black community. And by mentioning them here I don't mean to gloss over the many causes, which deserve to be, and have been, explored in detail in other books.)

Roland angered some people with a column calling on pastors to "stop having baby dedications for children until they have made an effort to meet with and involve the father in the life of the child." He says, "Now, here's why that's important. You go to these churches, and you have a string of women walking up. You have a mother, a grandmother, an aunt. That preacher should say, 'Who's the father? I need his phone number, address, e-mail, Twitter handle, whatever. We're going to send men from our youth ministry to go meet with him. Because we want to bring him in and say his responsibility is going to be in raising up the child.' And I think the pastors then need to deal with the relationship between the mother and the father, because whatever trials they might have, it needs to end when they think of the child." (Roland and his wife have raised his four nieces, who call him "daddy.")

Numerous campaigns are under way to improve things in the black community. And prominent voices like athletes LeBron James and Dwyane Wade are helping by speaking out about the issue. I'd love to see more media focus on great everyday dads who aren't famous, but happen to be black. Though one of them, Jay Ramsay, doesn't think that would sell.

"To be honest," Jay says, "What narratives are sexy? What grabs people's attention, reaffirms what they think of reality, and sells? The story of a black dad being like awful—yeah, I'll read that story. I don't want to read a story about people doing what they should."

"But doesn't the negative stereotype make you mad?" I ask.

"I don't know. All I know is I'm gonna take care of my kids until my last breath. I used to go to this Southern Baptist church. I would take my grandmother. And I remember this preacher, old Southern black guy, and he goes, 'Do you know why they keep searching out black men for guns, drugs, and illegal items?' The congregation doesn't say anything. He goes, 'Because they have them. That's why.' The reason why they think black men do this is because a lot do."

As a country, we should understand that both these things are facts: fatherlessness is a crisis especially acute in the black community, but most black fathers are good dads. While working on this book, I lost a good friend who was a fantastic, loving father. At his funeral at a black Baptist church, the preacher said, "At a time when fathers aren't being fathers, he was one of the good ones." I wanted to call out, "Most are!" But I didn't.

Some dads have found that these low expectations lead them to get more praise than they deserve. "In the African American community, we have this whole thing about fatherhood. I got way too much credit," says Ta-Nehisi Coates, who has written and spoken out about fatherhood.[6]

Doyin Richards, whose photo of himself wearing one kid in a carrier while doing his other daughter's hair went viral, speaks for dads of all races. "I have a dream that people will view a picture like this and not think it's such a big deal," he wrote on his blog. "Somewhere there's a dad doing the exact same thing for his daughters. Somewhere there's a dad who put his foot down with his boss and refused to attend an 'urgent staff meeting,' so he could leave work early to attend his daughter's dance recital. Somewhere there's a single dad successfully getting his three sons ready for school."[7]

If the photo had shown his wife doing the same thing, "Many would probably think it's cute, but after ten seconds of looking at it, they would probably move on to the next shiny object on their newsfeed. Why? Because it just wouldn't be a big deal to many people if a woman did it."

Maybe the answer is for us dads to post lots of these pictures all over the web until people get bored of them and come to understand that it's fully normal for a dad of any race to do basic caregiving. Then maybe the Neanderthals and other stragglers who haven't gotten the memo on modern manliness will start to feel left out, try doing these things as well, and see how rewarding it is.

Or perhaps there's a more powerful antidote that could shock uninvolved fathers into realizing what they're missing and changing their ways. That's what one former absentee dad turned NFL dad thinks. For this book, he decided he's ready to divulge his story.

Confessions of an Absentee Dad Turned NFL Dad

He began as a stand-up guy and hands-on father. Reggie Ball was a military man, hardworking and committed to his family. But within a few years, he became an absentee father and serial impregnator. Now this former Marine and police officer, currently a personal trainer and football coach, has spent years repairing his relationships with his six kids, including two who made it into the NFL.

In an interview, Reggie decided to open up about his entire story. He has a message for absentee dads around the country and ideas for guiding them to do the right thing. Here's Reggie's story, in his own words:

I was born the fifth of six kids. My mom and dad were together, always working. My brother raised us. They worked at Rich's department store. My dad was a supervisor in the bakery; my mom worked on the apparel floor. We lived in a small house downtown. I shared a bed with one of my older brothers. It was hell. He would punch you if you touched him. He took all the covers, and it was cold. I would get up in the middle of the night and sleep in a pile of clothes, just so he wouldn't punch me. It was a chain of command.

We were poor, but as kids we didn't know it. We thought everybody ate chicken and rice every night. Mama would make ribeye. Mama would come home at 6:00. Dad came home at 11:00. You'd see him when you were "supposed to," so he could tell you to clean the kitchen, mop the floor. That's why I'm still paranoid about kitchens and bathrooms being clean. In our first house, when you left food on the table, you had rodents, and you could hear them.

Then we moved to Decatur. In our new house, we thought we were *The Brady Bunch*. Shag carpet? We'd never been to a house with carpet. We had a door. We thought we were *Leave It to Beaver* with twin beds. We thought we had made it. We felt rich. The kitchen was totally separate. Every room was separate.

We had been at an all-black school. Now we were at a predominantly white school. Words were pronounced differently. It was culture shock.

Sometimes we'd have fun with dad. Every year he took us to the great Christmas tree at Rich's department store. We'd ride the "pink pig," eat Thanksgiving dinner. The following day we would always go to the Georgia Tech–Georgia game. And every Sunday he'd take us to the park. In high school, he came to some of my football games when he wasn't working. Mom didn't. She didn't want me to play. It was too violent for her. It was nonsense to them. They wanted us to get an education and a good job.

I got good grades until adolescence. Then, girls. My parents tried to get me to stop running around, but the minute you tell a teenager what not to do, that's what they'll do.

When I graduated, I wanted to go to the army for two years, then police school. I got delayed entry into the military, so I worked at a Pike Nurseries to make money. Then my girlfriend of two years found out she was pregnant. I hadn't been that careful, but I was still surprised. I decided, "Okay, I'll take it head-on." So I enlisted and said, "Let me get you settled before I go to boot camp, because I have to have a foundation." I thought I was gonna be a man and prepare. We got married right after boot camp. Then I left again for infantry training school. We moved to Norfolk.

When I saw my son for the first time, it was surreal. That was part of me, right there. My dad was really upset, because he knew the struggle. He had a saying: "You're just gonna do it the dumb way. The rest of your life you're gonna be strong, but dumb. You'll be working on railroads and picking up transmissions instead of doing it the smart way, planning ahead." I never listened to him. But in a lot of ways he was right.

After I held my boy that first time, I stepped up—to making money, taking responsibility, every aspect of our life. "I gotta take care of this guy," I thought. I changed diapers, was hands-on from the beginning. When I would leave the room, he would cry.

A year and a half later, we had another son. Then two years after that, a third. I felt kind of overwhelmed, but good about my position. In the military I had all the medical insurance, so I didn't feel the bite another dad would. It worked out. It was tough. I was military police, and the budget was tight.

I came home once from working four days straight. When I opened the door, one kid screamed and cried. I wasn't sure if it was the uniform I was wearing, but I thought, "I want to be home every day. My kid doesn't know me." So I didn't reenlist. My colonel asked me, "What are you gonna do with three kids?" And I said, "I'm gonna live." I'll never forget what he said: "Don't ever be afraid to fail."

If I had reenlisted, I would have gotten $24,000 up front. I said, "I don't care. I don't want to miss them growing up." So we decided to move home. I filled out job applications and got a job at First Atlanta Bank, corporate security. I got out of the military April 8. On April 9 I had a job.

But then I started acting eighteen or nineteen years old again.

I was hanging around with single guys and other women. I had affairs. After seven years of marriage, my wife filed for divorce. I said okay. I got served papers at my mom's house. I didn't show up for divorce court. It was the dumbest thing I did in my life. So for the next two years, I was wandering aimlessly from house to house, seeing my kids on occasion.

I could have solved it and seen my kids if I wanted to. But I thought that the world was mine, and, "They're kids, they'll be all right." That was bullshit.

A few years later, I was dating another girl, got serious, and thought this was it. We got married the year our son was born and had another son four years later. But the promiscuity was still there.

Why would I get married if I still wanted to sleep with other women? That's the million-dollar question. My wife didn't like it, but what broke that camel's back was that during one of my outings, I impregnated another woman. My wife found out and confronted me. I denied it. She went off.

I wasn't using condoms. I just kept thinking it wasn't going to happen to me again. It's so ignorant. I thought I'd use the "pull out" method, and I carried around contraceptive foam. Once I ran out of that, I just didn't bother with anything. I was so arrogant, so full of myself. After my first three kids I didn't want more kids. I thought about getting a vasectomy, but honestly I thought it would take away from me, change me.

Throughout all this, I was making the child-support payments. With this last pregnancy, I told my girlfriend, "I can't buy you a sandwich. I'll do what I can." So she mostly raised my daughter.

I kept on living in cheap houses. Still promiscuous, but at a different rate. I started using condoms all the time. And I carried around the morning-after pill. I would hand it to the women.

I'd see my kids sometimes and go to their games. But I wasn't really in their lives. I started a landscaping business and was making money. I'd pay the child support. I became just a check, just money to the women.

Then I met Lyn. She had a boy and a girl. We hit it off. I told her, "I should have married you." She said, "You weren't ready, you were such a big whore." It was like right after I left the Marine Corps, somebody had taken a mask off of me and I could finally breathe. And now Lyn kicked the last of that out of my system.

She came down to where I was working as a personal trainer. She brought with her the girl I was cheating with. And the look in Lyn's face, the hurt, it hurt me so bad. I said, "If I ever get out of this, I'm done."

It took a year and a half before I could even touch her again, even though we slept in the same bed. It's been more than ten years. And our relationship is perfect now. I go home every night. We're together all the time now. She can answer my phone. She can look at my phone.

In their teens, her kids started looking at me like a father. Their dad wasn't around. He was to them what I was to my kids. And that's when it really hit me: "Shit, what about my kids?" I pulled back a bit from Lyn's kids, because I felt guilty. And I started reaching out to my kids.

I'd call, and the responses I got were cold, cold, cold. It was like throwing pieces of bread to a tiger. I'd say, "Let's go to the park." If I could get two or three of them, any of them, it didn't matter. They'd say, "Eh, we'll call you back." Click. Until, eventually, they started to say, "Okay." I didn't want to disappoint them any more than I already had.

I also started seeing this problem in a bigger way. I started coaching football and saw a room full of kids who were raising themselves. Young boys who didn't have their dads. Wayward young black males, saying shit, with unbridled mouths. They needed structure and fathers.

My oldest son, Reggie, was in my first class. I coached him from tenth to twelfth grade. We had a cordial relationship. He would give me a look. I would always tell him, "If I've done something to you, I'm sorry. I can't change that."

My kids would give it to me. They'd say, "You weren't here, who the fuck are you, don't tell me shit," stuff like that. The kids each had their own segue into telling me how they felt. And that was hard to swallow. But I did it and listened. I just took it.

The narcissistic part of me, the alpha male, wanted to say, "I'm your daddy. Don't get smart with me." I wanted all the garnishing of being a king, but I hadn't ruled over them or given them dadlike instructions. I just said, "I'm sorry."

It took years. A long time. But our relationships have totally changed. One of my boys, Reshawn, called me just the other day and said, "I'm so glad you're my dad. I love you, because a lot of guys don't have their dads. You did some shit I didn't like, but you made up for it now."

Reggie played in the NFL for a while, then got injured. Now he's coaching. We're two peas in a pod. I'm doing what I should have done when he was a teenager. We text and talk all the time. He just had a baby boy—he waited until he was thirty.

Marcus has a one-year-old. He signed with the New Orleans Saints. All my boys are big like me and play football. I teach them how to work out.

My boys are educated about sex, and they remember not having me. I told them, "I beg of you, don't breed on the first heat." I taught them how to use a condom. I used a cucumber. Moms asked why I gave them condoms. I said, "If you don't give them condoms, you gonna babysit."

I also took them to some bad areas of town. They'd say, "Dad, these people are nasty." I'd say, "This is where you'll be if you don't have an education when you have a house full of kids and can't pay for them. This is where you'll be."

To dads out there who are going around having all these babies, I say, "Get the fuck up. Take care of that." We need to teach kids to be selective in the breeding process. The timing has to be right. You have to have a foundation before you do all that. And if you messed up, get in that kid's life. If you can't spend money, spend time.

Here's what we need to do: have these absentee dads spend time with kids the same age as their kids. Kids who remind them of their kids.

And we should tell black men who ignore their kids, "You're the reason people don't trust us. Because you're not teaching these kids. You need to be out there spreading education. Help these kids. You're the reason their ass is showing down the street. When they put tattoos all over their body and can't get a fucking job, you're the reason. Tell them, 'Don't do that, because I did.'"

I regret the time I missed with my kids, talking to them, spending time with them, teaching them certain things. This, what I'm doing now, is much more fulfilling, more manly than what I used to do. When I was doing that, I felt numb. A couple times I was like a fucking actor. It was all fake. But love is effortless. It's effortless now to talk to my kids.

It's a thankless job, but I'll do it all day. I got friends who aren't particularly good dads and I chew their ass. I have a brother who just got out of jail, and I called him. His son walked past me and I smelled marijuana. I said, "It's not legal here, son, so if I stop you, it's probable cause. Asshole, stop it." I called my brother and said, "You gotta get in his life." He called me yesterday and said he's moving in with him next weekend.

I mentioned in the last chapter that I spent a day at a public housing project for an NPR story. Reggie, who's been a friend for years and knew the area from his days as a cop, insisted on coming along to

keep me safe, particularly given the expensive equipment I was carrying. He was moved and angered by what the residents said in the
interviews. In the car on the way back, he told me he wanted to yell at
some of the women to stop having all these babies they couldn't afford
and to stop counting on the government to somehow lift them out
of their situation when they continued having unprotected sex with
random men. One of the last women I interviewed was a pregnant
single mom with five kids. A beautiful boy, her two-year-old son,
with deep brown eyes, was sitting on her lap.

"Where do you think he'll be when he's sixteen?" I asked Reggie.

"I'll tell you exactly where he'll be. He'll be walking around these
streets with his shirt all the way open, some chain hanging around
his neck, never going to school, and dealing drugs. And at eighteen?
Probably a dad or in jail. Or both."

I've never forgotten that little boy, and I hope and pray for the best.
For this book, I decided to jump into the future and interview him
when he's eighteen—or the next best thing. I met up with a bunch
of men—some white, some black, most of them young—who have
ended up, as Reggie put it, "both."

Dads in Prison Open Up

E d's father left home before he can remember, taking his brother with him. Ed's mother, a drug addict, got into a violent relationship. "Her boyfriend beat her and hit her in the head," Ed says. As a little boy, he saw it happen. His mom suffered brain damage and began hearing voices. One day, she shot her own father. "Her voices told her he was harming me and my uncles," Ed says. Ed's grandfather took a bullet in the arm, survived, and raised him after his mom went to jail.

As a teen in northern California, Ed got into trouble of his own. Looking for camaraderie, he did drugs and followed some of his relatives into a gang—a white supremacist one. "It was so stupid," he says. He stole cars, got caught at age twenty, and went to jail for six years for grand theft auto. When he got out, he went to Montana, where his mom, then also out of jail, had settled.

Within months he got a girl pregnant, married her, and moved with her to Georgia to be near her parents. "I had a wife and daughter, needed money, but didn't know where to go," he tells me at his prison in Columbus, Georgia. "I started selling and buying." He was caught, charged with possession of illegal drugs, and sentenced to eight months behind bars.

Ed knows his background doesn't excuse the choices he made.

None of the dads I interviewed in prison can claim that, except maybe Joseph. He was born with fetal alcohol syndrome and never got treatment. Both his parents "drank themselves to death" when he was a kid, he says. His family gave him alcohol from the time he was a baby. He grew up alcoholic. As a kid, he missed a lot of school. "My early years? I really don't remember them," he says.

He's been in and out of jail since age twelve. Joseph's now fifty-two, but looks older. "It's always shoplifting, always," he says. When we met, he was incarcerated because he was accused of walking into a tool store and trying to steal. "I don't remember, I swear to God," he says. He only remembers employees on top of him. That wasn't unusual for him. "I walk around and don't know where I am." It's heartbreaking to speak with him. You can see the suffering in his eyes.

Joseph's struggle is emblematic of a problem at the heart of our criminal justice system. "Psychiatric disorders are the only kind of sickness that we as a society regularly respond to not with sympathy, but with handcuffs and incarceration,"[1] New York Times columnist Nicholas Kristof wrote, citing a study that found that half of U.S. prisoners have mental-health problems.[2] Joseph says he wants to be "rescued." He could go out walking one day and "end up dying on the riverbanks." More than anything, he wants a relationship with his daughter, who is now thirteen and being raised by her aunt. Her mother also had addiction problems.

"Do you love your daughter?" I ask.

"My God, yes, I do," Joseph says, his eyes welling up. "One day at time. That's all I can do." Joseph says he hasn't drunk alcohol or taken drugs for years. But he also hasn't had help with his disorder.

The other dads I spoke with at the Muscogee County Prison have no such excuse for their actions. But nearly all shared stories of fatherlessness, addiction, financial desperation, and kids they aren't raising. We spoke right after this group of nine inmates took part in Inside-Out Dad, a seven-week course created by the National Fatherhood

Initiative that teaches men how to be better fathers while incarcerated and after they get out.

The day I visited, Larry Washington was guest speaker. He's a local pastor and motorcycle enthusiast who sounds like Burl Ives in *Frosty the Snowman.* He told his own story of fatherlessness. Larry's grandfather died before his father was born. His dad grew up "dirt poor" in Mississippi, with a mother and six sisters, in a family full of alcoholics. At seventeen, his father was "saved" when a revival came through town. Larry's father spent his life traveling around the country knocking on doors and didn't raise his kids. When he came home, all he would do is "correct" Larry. "My dad would lay a belt on me," he said.

Larry grew up learning nothing about being a man or a father. When he got married and had kids, he was wrestling with addictions and internal struggles and wasn't much of a parent. "Most of us just grew up and ended up with kids, and the vast majority of us don't know what to do," he says of the men in the room. "We ain't got a clue."

But in later years, something big happened to Larry. "My dad was broken. He looks at me and says, 'I am so sorry I have failed you as a father.' It didn't seem like a big thing at the moment, but forgiveness breaks the bondage. My whole perspective gradually began to change. And over the years, my father became the father that all of us would want to have. I began to see he never intended to hurt me. Wanting to hurt, kill, hate him was all wrong."

Larry changed as well. "If you recognize your failures, if you come face-to-face with them and acknowledge your struggles and deal with them, you can change your heritage. You can be a father who was there. You can be a father who made a positive influence."

Larry's message to the men in this room is clear: let go of the anger over your past; forgive, so you can move on and build a better life. That means learning how to have good, healthy, respectful relationships at home, with a wife and children, he said. "If you don't, you're headed for some big heartaches in life."

Larry committed to building relationships with his own kids. "Now about every three weeks I get a tape of the 'Daddy and Daughter Show'—videos of my son with his daughter. Every time, I smile. I know that's a piece of me."

Some weeks, the InsideOut Dad program is more about instruction. Dads learn ways to communicate with their children and questions to ask. They practice how to really listen. They learn to write letters to their kids, what to say and not say.

"Graduation is the greatest and most painful day of the entire process," says Neil Richardson, the prison chaplain who administers the program. "There's excitement for the future, but these men are confronting their pain over all the time they've missed being the best dads they can be." Often, families come to watch.

The program is working. Overall, recidivism rates at this prison are about 66 percent, Richardson says. Among the InsideOut Dad participants, it's half that. Since these men are choosing to take part in the program, they're ready to change before they start. So it's unclear how much of the credit goes to the program. But Richardson says it makes a huge difference.

"They're forming bonds here and keep forming them. One of our graduates now takes his daughter to the library for hours at a time every week. We know two things are happening: she isn't going to end up here, and he isn't coming back." In his years working in the prison system, Neil says, he and others have found that six out of ten kids whose parents don't read to them will end up in jail when they grow up.

The InsideOut Dad program works in part by equipping men to withstand temptations they'll face when they get out. By building relationships with their families, they'll have a better chance of ignoring the criminals who will try to reel them back in. "When a guy walks out of here to his old neighborhood, probably the first person who will greet him isn't a family member. It's a 'friend' who will say, 'Hey, here's a little something something'—drugs. And, 'There's a girl waiting for you.' Three hours later, he'll knock on the door and say, 'It's time to start.'"

Anytime we hear statistics about struggling single moms and fatherless kids, we need to remember that the vicious cycle of poverty, lack of education, drugs, incarceration, and recidivism is part of it. U.S. prisons hold about 750,000 fathers and 65,000 mothers.[3] A little more than 2 percent of children have a parent behind bars. And the percentage of parents in jail is growing.[4]

More than four in ten incarcerated fathers are black. Among mothers, it's almost three in ten.[5] Of the nine men in the InsideOut Dad program on the day I visited, six were black. One, named Keith, never knew his father. His mother went to jail for cocaine possession when he was seven, and he grew up in several different foster families. After high school, he tried to live with his mom, but her boyfriend, who did drugs, didn't want Keith around. Soon he got two young women pregnant, started selling drugs to make money, and was caught.

Speaking with a stutter he's had since birth, Keith told me Inside-Out Dad is teaching him about "being a role model." He says, "When I get out, I want to go back to school, get a job, spend time with my daughters."

Another inmate, Dennis, was raised mostly by his grandmother, though his mother and stepdad—"an alcoholic, but a good man"— were still in his life. He got into trouble for selling stolen merchandise and says the latest accusation put him in prison awaiting a hearing. He says he's determined to turn his life around for his children. "It hurts when my daughter says, 'You told me you'd come and get me. Why didn't you?' She doesn't know I'm in prison. I say, 'I'm at work.' She says, 'All you do is work.' And my son, I want to be at his next birthday. I've missed all his birthdays. I have to be there now. It's not a choice. I have to."

Joseph, who is white, will likely never be able to hold down a job because of his medical condition. But he has a simpler dream: "For my daughter to be standing outside those doors when I walk out. And to sit down and let me to explain to her one-on-one what I've done, that I'm an addict, that I've done wrong. That's all I want."

InsideOut Dad is one of two programs run by the National Fatherhood Initiative to help get dads connected to their kids, even when they can't be there. The other is for a group of dads who have done nothing wrong, and everything right.

How Military Dads Are
Staying Connected

The images make just about everyone cry. Videos of dads home from war surprising their kids at school are wildly popular, and for good reason. The screams of excitement and relief, tears, and hugs are a powerful reminder of what America's military families go through.

Nearly half of U.S. service members are parents, most of them fathers.[1] More than a third have kids younger than six.[2] And in many of those families, dad or mom has gone through multiple deployments to war zones in Afghanistan or Iraq.

I love the homecoming videos and have shown some on TV. But they only tell part of the story. What happens when those initial days of jubilation are over? How can a man reintegrate into his family with any sense of parental authority when he's been gone so long?

"They may be commanding a battalion in the field, and then they come home and can't even tell their own kids what to do because that's mom's job," says Vince DiCaro, who helped spearhead the program at the National Fatherhood Initiative. "It creates a lot of tension."

These dads are also often going through emotional turmoil and in many cases suffer from PTSD, making their challenges that much tougher. "When I came home from the Marine Corps, I really had a hard time adjusting to it," one dad told a group of researchers.[3] "Coming from a structured lifestyle, being told what to do, how to do it, when to do it, to coming home and being a full-time dad, and everything else. I didn't know how to adjust to it . . . And I didn't spend as much one-on-one time with my daughter as I should have. I'm still learning."

Many said their experiences at war made parenting harder, and they "perceived a need to build their own capacity to express emotions and provide nurture to their children," the study found. They also need to learn to manage their tempers. One man said he gets stressed very easily, and when his daughter stomps and cries, he feels like "grabbing her, if I have to drag her to her room and just leave her there." He wants to learn better ways to handle those moments.

Some of these children are so young they don't even know their dads, so the fathers find themselves trying to build relationships from scratch when they arrive home from a long deployment. These kids see their mother as their only parent. So the National Fatherhood Initiative put together a program to help military fathers build close relationships with their kids even when deployed.

I interviewed Lieutenant Commander Dennis Albert Kelly of the U.S. Navy, who has done five deployments, four of them in war zones, including Iraqi waters. He has five kids at home in Texas. He grew up without a father—and, in his teen years, without a mother as well. He's committed to being involved in his kids' lives even while his service takes him far away. And, as a navy chaplain, he works with other men who are struggling to do the same. He spoke via Skype from Bahrain. Here are his words:

I have no idea who or where my dad is. He wasn't in my life as a kid. My mother was married a number of times, so there was kind of a parade of men in her life. I had no real father figures. Most of the men were just interested in my mom, and us kids were just an unfortunate side effect of being with her. I have an older brother from a different dad. I think my younger brother and I have the same dad.

In high school, one of my stepdads died. My mom left the country. She would come home and put food in the refrigerator once a month. I found out eventually she was coming in to pick up her Social Security check. She was in Jamaica.

A friend's parents took my younger brother in, and another friend's parents took me in. That's when I saw what a real dad looked like. He stood up for me as my dad at my wedding.

I was the first in my family to graduate from high school. I went to college on a ROTC scholarship. My mom paid for the first year of college with money from my stepdad who died. She spent the rest. I got a masters in chaplaincy, and now I'm studying for a doctorate. I never did drugs or alcohol. A lot of it has to do with God's grace, his hand in guiding me. My brothers had all kinds of issues. With marriage, I recognized I had no clue. So I started reading books on what it means to be a godly husband, godly father. I got married at twenty-three and now have five kids.

Obviously it's hard to be apart from them. I cope with it by knowing what I do is meaningful. It's a sacrifice I'm willing to make. As a father, the key is intentionality. A lot of guys just put it on hold. That doesn't work. I have family time scheduled into my day. Before FaceTime and Skype, I'd write letters. Now there's the technology. The biggest thing I do is read to them.

Through this program, you read books to your kids over video and either record it on a DVD, if there's no connectivity where you are, or send it by e-mail. I just finished the first of a *Mary Poppins* series with my twins—they turn five this week. I finished a third Narnia book with my middle two, and I'm reading Nancy Drew with my oldest. They each get their own story. The Wi-Fi can be sketchy, so it doesn't really work to read the books live. I send them recordings. But we talk live. I talk with them at the end of their day, my morning, and vice versa—both. They bookend my day.

This is my first time stationed in Bahrain, and it's nicer than before, because I can do more parenting. My oldest son can carry the iPad to another room, and we can talk about things he just did. I tell dads to schedule time to do this, write letters, make videos, do arts and crafts—the kind of stuff you would do with them if you were home. So they know they're important.

Still, it's complicated when I go home after each deployment. A lot of it is about a handoff with mom. It's a dance you've got to do to integrate yourself. It's not the way it was when you left. A lot of things have changed—rules, room situations. Jumping in and being the authoritative dictator is a recipe for disaster. And it happens a lot among military dads, unfortunately. I try to take it slow and not throw my weight around. The kids are caught in the middle, and it disrespects my wife for me to come in and start changing things.

Sure, I wish I wasn't away. The last couple of weeks especially have been hard on my wife. There's flooding in the house; one twin has double pneumonia, the other has acute bronchitis, and my older son has acute bronchitis too. Car troubles, and anything else that can go wrong has.

It goes back to meaning and purpose. When I feel that what I'm doing is no longer valuable, then I'll go home. I was a finalist for the Military Fatherhood Award from NFI, but don't feel that I should be an exception. The things that I do every dad should do. Being a dad is not being a babysitter, and not extraneous. You are uniquely qualified for that job. My oldest son and I, we do Cub Scouts together. I've been his den leader. Another family has taken him on while I'm away. When the dad from that family was in Afghanistan, I did the same for his two boys. We fill the gaps.

It's a big thing that the military has gotten more conscious about all this. We've realized we've got to do something about it. Family is part of who a military service member is. As a chaplain, I work with service members to process all sorts of things, and this is part of it.

Even though I'm forty, I have a five-year-old kid, which puts me right alongside some of the twenty-five-year-olds in the military. I have the chance to serve as a model, and a role model. Fatherhood is my life. I don't know that it's something I dreamed about, but by the time we had our first, I'd gotten excited about it. We'd been trying for several years. Still, it is a little bit terrifying. People say your daughter will grow up to marry a man like you. That's humbling. So I want to be the kind of husband I want my daughter to marry and the kind I want my sons to be.

When I spoke with Dennis, he was looking forward to heading home in November—and would deploy again in December.

There are also, of course, many deployed moms who are going through these same struggles. Fortunately, there are programs for them, and many of these same programs from the National Fatherhood Initiative work equally well for women. And parents left at home raising the kids, often the moms, have unique struggles as well. I interviewed a group of military moms at a military installation for a CNN show on the economy. I was struck by their stories of raising multiple children alone on very little money. It's a form of heroism. You can see this and learn more about these programs at the website for this book.

As we think about changes needed to improve parenting in America, let's not forget: the fewer the wars, the more kids have their parents.

Courts, Custody, and "Deadbeat Parents"

S ome dads are forced into the role of absentee father by being torn from their kids in bitter custody battles. The stereotypes and stigmas we've discussed make those battles worse. Creating caregiving laws and policies that are fair to both sexes will go a long way toward alleviating this struggle, which hurts great moms and dads and, most importantly, children.

There's a widespread perception that courts are still unfair to dads in deciding custody. This perception leads some dads to not even fight for custody, because they assume they'll lose in a biased court system. Some legal experts insist, however, that that's now just a myth. "Although it has not always been so, today's courts will generally award custody to whichever parent would be in the best interests of the child," the legal website FindLaw says.[1]

But some parents and attorneys say the legal picture isn't really this rosy. "From a legal perspective, most courts are obligated to focus on the best interests of the child. However, the reality is that a gender bias exists due in large part to the antiquated notion that women make better parents," family-law attorney David Pisarra said in a *Huffington Post* column.[2]

There's no way to get hard numbers on this. I can tell you that one in four kids lives with just one custodial parent and that that parent is the dad 18 percent of the time—very low compared to moms, but a huge jump from previous generations.[3] But these figures don't tell us how many dads *wanted* to be the custodial parent or how many put up a fight for custody.

Most cases don't involve court battles. The parents work it out themselves. "When it came time for my ex and me to begin to dissolve our marriage, the first thought we had was that neither one of us wanted to keep the kids away from the other," says Doug French, dad of two in Detroit. "We just didn't want to be married anymore."

When it is up to courts, shared custody is becoming more of a norm. A group of researchers in Wisconsin did an in-depth analysis of custody cases in the state. In a set of cases they looked at, in the 1990s moms got sole custody 60 percent of the time. By 2007, that was down to 45 percent. Shared custody, meanwhile, jumped from 15 to 30 percent. But the amount of the time that kids were placed solely or primarily with their dads barely changed, remaining below 10 percent.[4]

To keep things moving in the right direction, we need to put an end to an argument that's often used in custody battles: since moms generally spend more time in caregiving activities, they should get full or primary custody. In the *Huffington Post*, "divorce coach" Cathy Meyer argues, "It only makes sense that mothers who have a closer bond due to the time spent caring for a child be the one more likely to retain primary custody after a divorce."[5]

This argument is based on a widespread misunderstanding of what "working moms" and "working dads" do. No need to rehash it all here. But as I explained in the Introduction, moms and dads generally work equally hard on behalf of their families. With dads, more of those hours are more often in the office. Extra work hours necessary to keep a job and pay the mortgage are part of parenting. This should never be an argument in favor of taking a parent's children away from him or her.

Now that roles are shifting, more women are starting to face this same problem. "Men are now able to argue that they spend more time with the kids than their working wives do," divorce attorney Raoul Felder told *Working Mother* magazine. "This is one of the dark sides of women's accomplishments in the workplace—they're getting a raw deal in custody cases, while men are being viewed more favorably."[6] A response came from writer Lisa Belkin in the *New York Times:* "Is it not, in effect, the same presumption—the parent who works harder parents less—that men have faced for years?"[7]

But there's another wrinkle that's based on society's skewed expectations of men and women. Working women are often held to a higher standard as parents. Some managers think these women should be home and that men should be at work. Some courts may hold this same bias. So some legal experts fear that women may be punished for working just as many hours as men. If a woman works, let's say, forty-five hours a week, a judge may decide that's too much for a woman and that she has lost her right to equal custody; but if a man works forty-five hours a week, the same judge may decide he deserves equal custody. This is yet another reminder of the importance of eradicating the backward thinking that's hurting both women and men.

Custody battles are only part of the story. What tears many dads away from kids isn't the final custody decision, but what happens in the months or years before custody is determined. Several friends of mine who are great fathers were forcibly separated from their children. In some cases, their ex-wives or soon-to-be ex-wives wouldn't let them enter their former homes to take the kids or took the kids away and didn't say where. These dads got no immediate relief from courts.

One man I know, a fantastic, loving father who lives on the West Coast, faced an even worse nightmare: his wife falsely accused him of sexual abuse. It made no sense, because in custody proceedings she had repeatedly argued that he did not spend enough time alone with their daughter. When a court didn't award her what she wanted, she invented the sexual abuse charge, alleging an incident years earlier.

"I wasn't allowed to see my daughter without supervision. I had to pay for these trained supervisors who would come to my house before my daughter. Her mom would drop her off and make sure the person was there. And I would get one hour," this dad says. "I also had to pay for a psychometric test. It cost about $1,500. They hooked up wires to me, showed me all these pictures of naked boys and naked girls, and asked, 'Does this arouse you?' Actually, it traumatized me."

He is hardly alone in undergoing this. But it is important for courts to be vigilant in investigating all claims of sexual abuse. The Leadership Council on Child Abuse and Interpersonal Violence reports that 6 percent of custody cases involve allegations of sexual abuse, and investigators determine that about half are true. And in most cases where the abuse is not substantiated, "the allegations were believed to have been made in good faith and based on genuine suspicions."[8]

Some abusers try to get custody of their children, and our society has to do what it can to weed them out. As I mentioned earlier, government figures show that most child abuse is carried out by women, but most sexual abuse is done by men. So it makes sense that these situations in custody battles would affect fathers far more often than mothers.

I asked this dad on the West Coast why, he thinks, his ex fought so hard against sharing custody when everyone knew what a great father he is. "I don't have the answer to that. I think it's twofold. Because she is the mom, she gets a certain higher status—don't ask me why—and she likes that. And she's got money from her family. The attorneys saw that and knew she could keep spending. They'll push you to keep going when you can keep paying. A lot of it is who can hold on the longest. I cleared out my 401(k)."

A leading attorney who focuses on helping dads in these kinds of cases suggests a solution. "Close law schools—too many law schools, too many lawyers," says Chantale Suttle, who runs the firm Dadvocacy. "Lawyers don't make the pie bigger, they just cut it into smaller slices."

Although she means it, that's also partly tongue-in-cheek. Chantale knows law schools are a matter of supply and demand. What she really wants is for far more couples to realize that extended divorce and custody battles are egged on by a financial system that's bad for them and their children. The more people realize this, the fewer will let some avaricious attorneys manipulate them. "I'm a parental equality lawyer," she says. "I just feel dads have a harder time getting there. This isn't about a gender war. We need a war against the system trying to perpetuate itself—high-priced lawyers trying to find a reason to exist."

Chantale created the firm after having "a Jerry Maguire moment." "I realized," she said, "that my husband and I couldn't afford to divorce if we wanted to. Holy cow! We make pretty decent money compared to most people. I couldn't afford to pay me what I charge. So now I'm a flat-fee lawyer, which is very unusual in Florida. My clients are mostly in nonmarital situations.

"The laws are written gender-blind, but the application falls in favor of the mother even when the parties are similarly situated. I have a client whose wife wouldn't let him take the kids. He texts his wife that he's picking them up from school and keeping them for the weekend. She calls the police, files a restraining order, and gets a mercy hearing." Chantale wants laws establishing that when there's a custody dispute, it's split fifty-fifty until a resolution is worked out in court.

"When I get the call, 'She didn't let me see my kids,' my heart is broken for the child, who goes, 'Why didn't daddy come?' He's got his shoes on, his backpack, and he can't wait to tell dad about something. My kids are seven and nine years old. When I traveled for a weekend, I talked and Skyped with them six times in forty-eight hours. I can't imagine not being allowed to be there.

"If I could pick one word to describe the five hundred men I've met over the last year and a half, it's 'defeated.' And by the way, a lot of moms who wouldn't let dads visit when the kids were little, when the teenage years come, they're like, 'They're all yours.'"

Many dads live with the fear in the back of their mind that if their marriage fell apart, they could lose access to their children. "I would love to see laws that give us rights over our children," says Jay Ramsay. "If my wife and I got divorced, the court would side with her—unless I have evidence against her. I don't have any rights. I guess some male lawmakers thought, 'No, the kids are really the woman's problem.'"

But dads who have won full custody prove that's not always the case. "I feared what environment my daughter would be in with her mother," says one man I interviewed who has raised his daughter alone. "I knew there would be multiple men passing through. My wife was a stay-at-home mom, so while I fought for custody I was paying my attorney bills and hers. I was adamant that my daughter not be raised in an unproductive place. Ultimately, multiple family psychologists said yes, 'Dad's is the better place to be. He's more stable.' I quit my job and opened up my own business from home. My ex tried to claim abuse, and the female judge saw through it."

Still, he believes family courts remain tilted against men. "It was luck of the draw that we got our judge. In family court, a woman can be a drug abuser, a murderer, and they'll still say mom is better. Things are improving for fathers, but a lot still get hosed over."

Sometimes, the dad shouldn't get even partial custody. A female friend of mine in Massachusetts would have loved to share custody with her ex-husband rather than handle the kids herself, but his home and the women he was shacking up with were inappropriate for children. I was relieved when she fought hard for, and won, full custody.

Once custody is determined, there's another problem that needs to be addressed—one that has some states currently taking actions that seem downright unconstitutional. It's the twisted world of custody payments and alleged "deadbeat dads."

"My original job out of law school was to enforce the child support system. I was the prosecutor," Chantale says. "I thought I was on the side of the angels. I was helping moms and kids. I was seeing dads rip up their paycheck and eat it rather than give it to the mom.

"We would go after the nonpayers, the nonsupporters. Then I made it to the bench, and my job was to be neutral. At the same time, I could see that the child-support landscape was vastly changing, because somewhere it became a game of numbers. The more money the government gets, the more it has for other entitlement programs. They figured out that it's easier to go after the dads already paying than the deadbeats. So it became about increased support and paying for kids older than eighteen."

Several states have incarcerated parents—the vast majority of them dads—for not paying the full amount of required child support, with no legal representation and no consideration of the ability to pay. "Everyone agrees that parents must support their children. But sending parents to jail for child-support debt just because they are poor is bad policy for children and families," the Southern Center for Human Rights says. Some states force "indigent parents who owe child support debt to plead for their liberty, without counsel, against an experienced, state-funded lawyer who is trying to send them to jail."[9]

In Florida, Chantale has seen heartbreaking cases. "I saw a dad with a port coming out of his chest. He couldn't pay because he was in chemotherapy. I had a guy in front of me who was in shackles on Christmas Eve. He wasn't the dad. He was the child's namesake. It was a mistake. All the mom has to do is complete a sworn affidavit that he's in arrears. The state will suspend his driver's license and his passport."

Nothing excuses a father who is refusing to pay child support when he has the money or just isn't trying to make money his kids need for basic expenses. Just like all the good fathers across America, I can't imagine ever doing that.

It's unclear how many dads have plenty of means to pay child support and just don't. The Urban Institute found that 4.5 million dads had no good reason for shirking this responsibility, while 2.5 million were poor. But those figures date all the way back to the late 1990s.

Also, the institute says that although poverty is no excuse for avoiding parental responsibility, "society devotes considerably more resources to helping poor mothers succeed in the labor market than it does to helping poor fathers do so."[10]

There's another important piece of this puzzle that gets little attention: deadbeat moms. When men get custody, they live without the full amount of child support they're supposed to receive just as often as women do. Only four out of ten moms and dads get the full amount they're owed.[11]

About half the custodial parents get all the money they're due when the kids have contact with the other parent. When there's no contact, custodial parents only get about 30 percent.[12] Of course, there are far more custodial moms than dads. And even among custodial parents, far fewer men are even supposed to receive child support. About half the custodial moms and a quarter of custodial dads have child-support arrangements.

In one way, deadbeat moms have an even worse track record than deadbeat dads. In the latest annual figures available, custodial moms received 63 percent of the child support they were due. Custodial dads got 56 percent.[13] Bruce Ailion, a real estate broker who tried to get child support for more than a decade, told *U.S. News and World Report* that his ex-wife has been thrown in jail several times for not paying. Still, "I cannot collect child support," he said. "I really feel for the waffle-house waitress working two jobs" who's in a similar situation and even more in need, he said.[14]

Men and women can work together to fix these problems. Here are five steps we can take together:

1. *Learn the laws* in your state. Do they give both genders an equal shot at receiving custody?

2. *Publicize the numbers.* Obtain records that allow you to calculate just how equitable your state's court system is. Contact

law schools and not-for-profit groups that focus on these
issues. If you can demonstrate a pattern of custodial decisions
along gender lines, the media will pick it up—and judges and
legislatures will respond.

3. Educate couples you know who are getting divorced. Show
them this book and introduce them to the financial system that
tricks couples into pouring away their life savings.

4. Eradicate unconstitutional laws. Are alleged "deadbeats"
getting thrown in jail with no charges or representation? This
doesn't help anyone. Fight for better laws and the election and
appointment of fair judges. Discuss this issue at town-hall
meetings with state representatives and even before your state
legislature.

5. Support not-for-profit groups that work with parents to make
support arrangements that are commensurate with what they
can actually afford and/or need.

I also have a proposal. Let's evict the term "deadbeat dads" from
our jargon. "Deadbeat parents" is a step in the right direction, but
only if we limit it to those who have the money yet are refusing to
provide child support. When we're speaking in general terms, let's
just stick with "parents who owe child support."

And let's not forget that, although the money is important, it's far
more important for a parent to be in a child's life and to act as a
positive influence. Often, that can be achieved. There's another, much
more painful scenario we all hate to think about, but need to in considering policies that work for American families. For this book, a
childhood friend of mine who lost his wife decided to open up and
share his story.

Widowers and Motherlessness

The dad raising his kids alone is the setup for all sorts of Disney story lines—think *The Little Mermaid, Aladdin, Beauty and the Beast, Hannah Montana*. It's also a favorite of classic 1980s sitcoms, like *Full House, Diff'rent Strokes, Silver Spoons,* and *Blossom,* before the "Doofus Dad" phenomenon set in. But in real life, the solo father doesn't get a lot of attention.

Aaron Hart, who has four daughters in Portage, Michigan, became one when his wife finally succumbed to an illness she had struggled with on and off for years. "It was the thing most like what you see on TV. The monitor goes beep, beep, beep, and they kick you out and go in with the cart. It was just horrible," he says of the night Cat died. "There's nothing like it. I would have guessed I was stuck out in the hall for twenty minutes, but I think it was really an hour they were working on her. They asked if I wanted to go back in, and they were still giving her CPR. When I was there, they called it. Her mother was there too."

As tough as life can get for parents, nothing compares to the pain of that kind of loss. Aaron and Cat had been together nineteen years, ever since college.

"Eventually, I had to come back home that night. The kids were sleeping. I gathered them in my bedroom, and we were sitting on the floor. I had to tell them that their mom died. They had the reactions you'd expect—screaming, crying. All I could do was just be there for them. It's as bad as you think it would be. And there's a kind of loneliness there that's hard to explain to people," he says.

That was in late 2013. Cat had been treated frequently for an unexplained illness causing serious infections. She spent more than a hundred days in the hospital in 2012. "I figured that one of these days there would be an infection that there was no antibiotic for," Aaron says. "They were using the exotic antibiotics on her." Still, "at the end it was very, very sudden."

Both sets of grandparents were there in the days after Cat's death, but the house felt too crowded. "The kids needed space. You'd think you'd want that comfort, but you also need room. The grandparents understood that. They got a hotel room. I just sat with the girls a lot. The older ones slept on the floor; the twins slept with me. I wasn't sleeping much at all. Too many thoughts were going through my head."

Three million kids live with just their fathers. About 8 percent of American homes are led by single dads, up from just 1 percent in 1960.[1] In most cases, the mom is still alive. But there are about 83,000 widowers like Aaron raising children alone.[2]

For him, daily life quickly became more difficult than anything he'd imagined. "I had to get some help. I was doing everything. The older girls could get themselves up and get ready, but not the twins. I was leaving work early to get home, make dinner, keep up the house. They still had their kid activities. I was burning the candle on both ends. I could tell I was getting snippy and impatient. I was short-shrifting everyone by trying to be everywhere." Yet the kids needed time with him more than ever. "It's difficult to address all your kids' needs and feel you're doing it fairly. They're all going through their own struggles, with their mom's death and with their life in general."

One of Aaron's concerns was making sure his oldest daughter, a teenager, didn't feel like the "mom" of the house. "She's always very naturally maternal, and when Cat was sick it was something we had to watch very carefully, that she not put too much pressure on herself."

Aaron was fortunate to work for an understanding business that cut him some slack and gave him time off after Cat's death. Still, he soon had to go back to work. That meant seeking solutions that would allow him more quality time with his kids. "There are programs like after-school child care, but they're very expensive, and it's incredibly difficult to coordinate," he says.

"If I gave you a magic wand, what would you make happen to improve parenting life?" I asked.

"I'd make it a priority to have child care at the work site, or nearby," he said. "That would be tremendous. You've got to work somehow."

Cat's mother lives next door and helps sometimes, and other grandparents sometimes travel in to help. Still, it was all too much. Aaron determined that the best, most affordable move was to have a nanny a few hours each day after school. "That way I can come home and talk to the kids about their day, go through their homework. She stays until about 7:00 and cooks." Another benefit is that it makes his oldest feel that she doesn't have to babysit.

I asked Aaron whether he's taking care of himself throughout all this. The family has done some group therapy, and he read some helpful books, he says. He's picked up a habit that he knows isn't healthy long term, using drinks at night to relax. He calls it "self-medicating with alcohol." But he also makes sure to exercise often. "I want to stay as healthy as I can for my kids and set a good example for them. I shorten my workouts; I go a couple times a week at lunch, and I'm running more than I was before."

There are programs that offer some help to single parents, but Aaron says he has found that they aren't tailored for dads. "I think single mothers is the predominant idea. There are more groups of women helping women. And the language is very much mother-to-mother language." This is another way in which we as a nation can join together. We can build programs to help single dads and extend programs for single moms to include both genders.

Aaron has found a community of fellow widowers online. It's a safe space to talk about being a widower without being judged. "Sometimes it seems more socially acceptable to say you're divorced than widowed," he says.

Given his home life of taking care of kids and organizing grand-parents' visits, Aaron says he often "feels trapped between twelve-year-olds and sixty-five-year-olds." He speaks with friends, but "it's incomparable to the loneliness. The kids pick up on it. They want to help dad. How do you tell an eight-year-old that her hug isn't like her mom's hug? I try to be accepting of the way I feel. This is the life I have to deal with now. What's the other choice? There is none."

He isn't complaining, just describing. Aaron often smiles as he dis-cusses life with his kids. "My daughter in middle school just finished a musical. She said she had to get 'stage makeup,' but she wasn't being specific. So I ended up e-mailing the director and saying, 'You have to treat me like an idiot.' She gave me very specific instructions," he says, chuckling.

These moments have become more precious. "My oldest is taking driver's ed class. She'll be out of the house in a couple of years. I feel for the people in my situation whose children are much younger. I'd just be such a horrible person if I gave up on fatherhood. The best I can hope to be is a really strong male role model for them."

There are far more widowed women than men in the United States[3]—about 313,000 single moms.[4] Some lost their husbands to vio-lence or war. I often visit a CNN.com page that contains the names and, in some cases, photos of every service member who has died as a result of the wars in Iraq and Afghanistan.[5] I read about some of these men and women and think about them and their families. I've showed the site on air and believe it's essential to remember the sacrifices being made every day.

One of my most powerful experiences as a journalist was an NPR story that brought me to the family of a fallen soldier days after he died. "This is my James Kinlow box; it's my time capsule," Kinlow's widow, Daphne, told me,[6] her arms wrapped around a large cardboard box containing newspaper clippings and cards from people around the country. Daphne lit up when I asked her about James and what he was like. She told me what a warm, loving father he was.

The challenges facing parents like Aaron and Daphne need to be considered as we push for laws and policies that allow people to be good workers and actively involved parents. It would be a big loss for a business to miss out on the contributions of solo parents and a far worse loss if their children had no time with them. The more we build positive changes for work-life balance, the more America's solo parents will have access to the opportunities and flexibility they need.

Now it's time to talk about the absolutely most misunderstood part of modern parenting—the part that makes most of us parents in the first place. Next we tackle what just may be the biggest reality check of all.

PART V

Sex

The Truth About Parents and Sex

Want to infuriate activists and writers who push for gender equality? Not that you should, but if for any reason you do, here's an easy way. Publish an article about the challenges modern couples are facing in bed. Be sure to include sweeping conclusions based on outdated studies or even a total lack of evidence.

The *Wall Street Journal* and *New York Times* learned this the hard way recently. In 2013, the *Journal* published a piece about sex in marriage subtitled "What Happens When He Says 'More' and She Says 'No'":

> Increasingly, experts believe sex is a more emotional experience for men than for women. Men tend to express feelings with actions, not words. Unlike a lot of women, they probably don't have heart-to-heart chats with everyone from their best friend to the bus driver, and they often limit hugs and physical affection to their immediate family.[1]

The story focused on a man who said his wife rebuffs him 95 percent of the time. It then cited statistics about the frequency of sex in marriage—from an outdated study published in 1994.

Slate issued a response entitled, "The *Wall Street Journal*'s Solution to Sexless Marriages: Stereotype All Men and Women." The couple featured in the *Journal* piece had sexual incompatibility that "can't be explained away by gender stereotypes like masculine sexual needs and feminine frigidity," *Slate*'s Amanda Hess wrote. "In the real world, we have relationships with individuals, not statistical gender profiles. . . . An individual's sex drive can't be predicted to fall at any particular point on the gender spectrum."[2]

For the *New York Times*, the responses were perhaps even harsher, in no small part because of how prominently the *Times* played its piece. The cover story of the *New York Times Magazine*—one of the highest-profile placements in all of American journalism—asked, "Does a More Equal Marriage Mean Less Sex?" The writer, sex therapist Lori Gottlieb, brought global attention to a study that, she said, "went against the logical assumption that as marriages improve by becoming more equal, the sex in these marriages will improve, too. Instead, it found that when men did certain kinds of chores around the house, couples had less sex."[3]

The study she wrote about was published in the *American Sociological Review*.[4] Researchers divided up household tasks by what's traditionally masculine, such as taking out the trash or fixing the car, and traditionally feminine, like folding laundry or vacuuming. It found that men who do more "feminine" tasks have less sex. Not much less, mind you—just 1.5 fewer times per month than men who did more "masculine" tasks. Gottlieb then wrote about seeing this among couples she counsels and quoted some other therapists who had seen the same: women wanted their husbands to share chores equally, but when they did, their wives were less "turned on."

"Completely ridiculous," the *New Republic* wrote in a response column. Writer Isaac Chotiner noted something Gottlieb had mentioned in the piece—that this study was based on a reading of data from the 1990s and that all sorts of variables can throw its conclusion into question.[5]

Sheryl Sandberg brought this up in our interview. When couples divide responsibilities more equally, "families are happier, marriages are happier, and despite that terrible *New York Times* article based on outdated research, couples have more sex, not less sex," she said. That idea—that more equality at home yields more good times in bed— gained a lot of attention after a study found that "both women and men who 'work hard' also 'play hard.' Results show that wives and husbands who spend more hours in housework and paid work report more frequent sex."[6] The study did not divide things up by which tasks are more "masculine" or "feminine." And again, it was based on old data.

I set out to check this and find up-to-date figures about the sex lives of moms and dads. At first, I thought that might be impossible. If there were more recent figures, why wouldn't these articles have cited them? It turns out more recent figures do exist, but no one, apparently, had dug them up. They're inside the massive 2012 General Social Survey (GSS), conducted by the National Opinion Research Center at the University of Chicago, one of the most prominent and respected analyses of American behavior. So I spoke with the man who oversaw the survey and hired one of his assistants to crunch the numbers for this book.

Here's what we found. There is no notable sex spike or drop when guys do traditionally female chores. Among men who said they do the laundry at home, half said they have sex less than once a week, while the other half have sex once a week or more. Men who said their wives do the laundry said the same thing. There might be a tiny bit of a sex spike for some guys who said they cook. Half of them report having sex once a week or more, while less than half the guys (42 percent) who said their wives prepare the meals report having sex that often.[7]

Maybe back in 2002 there was a substantial sex bonus for guys who did this stuff. The GSS from that year shows that guys who said they cooked and did the laundry reported having sex more often—not less, as in the older figures the *New York Times* referenced. But by 2012, in the GSS, that difference was gone. Is that because egalitarian marriages became more of a norm, less exciting, and therefore less of a turn-on? We can only theorize.

These figures are about men and women in general. I wanted to know how often *parents* with kids at home have sex. Again, it turns out these figures are available in the General Social Survey.

The big takeaways: American parents are having less sex than they used to. Sexlessness among parents has doubled. But a sliver of the population keeps getting it on four times a week or more, no matter what's going on in society. Let's call them the Sex Wealthy.

In general, people have less sex as they get older, so we'll break this down by age groups. Just over half of parents up to age thirty-nine have sex one to three times a week. And this figure has been dropping steadily. Back in the 1990s, about two-thirds had sex this often. It's similar for older parents. Just under half do the deed every week, down from a bit more than half in the 1990s.

More than three in ten parents have sex one to three times a month. One in twenty parents up to age thirty-nine has sex zero to two times a year. That jumps to one in eleven parents in their forties. In both cases it's more than double what it was in the 1990s.

Meanwhile, 9 percent of young parents can't keep their hands off each other, knowing each other biblically four times or more every week. For parents in their forties, that figure is a still solid 7.5 percent. It all but disappears past age fifty.

I had guessed that couples might have more sex once their youngest child reaches an older age. With no midnight feedings and no little kids to come running in, I thought, maybe couples copulate again. Nope. The number of couples having sex weekly or monthly stays about the same. But as the youngest child gets older, more parents drop out of the Sex Wealthy category. And sexlessness jumps up to 10 percent when the kids are teens. Of course, by then, we're generally talking about older parents as well.

Want to know about oral sex? I've got that for you too, from another survey.[8] In their thirties, 70 percent of married men receive oral sex at least once every ninety days. Those figures drop each decade, down to 46 percent of men in their fifties and 25 percent in their sixties. The figures are similar for how often they give oral sex to their wives. Overall, "previously less common sexual behaviors such as oral and anal sex appear to have become more widely practiced" since the early 1990s.

It makes sense that people want some kind of map or chart to look at to gauge how their sex lives stack up. But it's up to each couple to determine what works best for them. "There's no way to quantify what's the right amount of sex to have," says sexuality counselor and author Ian Kerner. "I try to encourage couples to have sex at least once a week. It's helpful to keep testosterone flowing, keep yourself eroticized."

Anyone who thinks men don't talk openly about sex is in for a surprise. In speaking with dads for this book, I found most wanted to talk about it in very real terms. "It goes in cycles. Sometimes we will go at it every day, and then we go through stretches of nothing," Robert, of Yonkers, New York, wrote me.

"Sex life is good. It's not over the top, but I'm not stressing out over it," said Troy, in Missouri, who is raising seven children and stepchildren.

"Terrible," said Kipp, in New Jersey. He and his male partner barely have time for sex. "Same as for friendships," he says. "I'm barely able to see friends because of our overscheduled lives."

Brent, who's also part of a two-dad couple, said the same. "I saw sex life is on here," he said, pointing to a list of topics I was looking into. "That could be a whole lot better."

Brent looked a little uncomfortable, so I interjected. "That doesn't make you different from anybody else."

"I know," he said. "It's still hard to say."

"It's part of the irony of parenting," I said. "The thing that made us parents is the thing that takes a backseat."

"Well, not for us!" Brent said.

"Oh, right!" I responded. Oops.

One dad, Tim, answered with one word: "masturbation." A sex study also looks at that. "For those providing sexual health counseling to couples, it may be important to acknowledge male masturbation as a prevalent and somewhat frequent behavior, even among those who are married or in relationships," the report said, finding that the numbers hadn't really changed since a 1992 study.[9]

Sometimes the process of becoming parents makes sex less enjoyable. "For us, sex became really about, 'Get me a child now,'" says Adam, of New York. "We had some miscarriages and had to get into the science of it—which is jerking off in a closet. That was a monster stress in our lives."

It's not the most frequent topic of conversation, but today's dads do discuss sex without the stereotypical locker-room ridiculousness. Adam says he gets questions from men who read his fatherhood blog and from husbands of his female readers. Some say, "Hey, my wife thinks you're cool." Then these husbands ask him to write posts encouraging women "not to shut down." Others ask for advice on that front. To them he says, "Have conversations, be communicative, help out more than you're helping out, send her away for a spa weekend and take the kid on your own. If you don't have those kinds of resources, just take the kid and go to your mom's house for a day. Let her relax in your house by herself. Buy her a manicure and pedicure."

Of course, this goes both ways. Dads and moms are both stretched out—superhero parenting is exhausting! The busy schedules create what former Labor Secretary Robert Reich, now a professor at UC Berkeley, once labeled "Dual-Income No-Sex" couples.

How do you avoid this fate? Here are ten steps for men and women:

1. Date each other again. "A big part of what I do is focus on engaging in intimacy outside the bedroom," Kerner says. "A lot of studies show the importance of the ratio of positive to negative interactions outside the bedroom and still trying to attract your partner. Really simple things combined with sexual willingness can lead to desire."

2. Put away the phones. Kerner talks with couples about eliminating "a lot of the digital distractions that are part of the fabric of our lives. The time people spend engaging other people is time they could spend engaging their spouse."

3. Boost each other's egos. "The early years of a child's life can be the toughest" on a couple's sex life, Kerner says. Many women "don't feel sexy" after a birth, and many men face insecurities because of the traditional expectations placed on them, including earning money, Kerner says. "They can feel depressed and have low self-esteem," which affects sexual desire. Make each other feel sexy, and good things will follow.

4. Care for your body. Taking care of yourself, exercising, and eating right all help with self-esteem and sexual desire, Kerner says.

5. Find moments for intimacy. Especially in the earliest months of a child's life, "intimacy that would normally be transferred between the couple is being transferred to the child," Kerner says. Sometimes, parents feel frustrated or angry about that. So it's important to carve out time for intimate connections even without sex.

6. Use erotica. Couples can do things outside the bedroom to spark desire, Kerner says. "Fantasizing together" and using "erotica or erotic stimuli" can help kick the sex life out of neutral and back into drive.

7. Schedule intercourse. "It's not uncommon for one week with no sex to become two weeks, a month, and then he's masturbating in the den and maybe she's masturbating in the bedroom," Kerner says. But if a couple schedules sex and tries to generally go to bed at the same time, sexual experiences return. "When couples start having orgasms again, they say how much they missed that."

8. Go through the motions. "One of the major complaints I have from couples is they're too tired to have sex," Kerner says. "Sometimes if they put their bodies through the motions, the mind will follow. It's important to have sexual willingness even though they're not in the mood. There's a state before arousal. With an overtaxed couple you can't expect desire to just manifest."

9. Reposition to reinvent. To make sex feel less mechanical and more exciting, try doing it a new way. "Reposition sex to be fun, creative, and novel," Kerner says. "If couples find sex boring, then more than likely they haven't reinvented sex."

10. Talk about it. Having frank conversations about sex is important, Kerner says. The youthful bluster that leads teens and twenty-somethings to lie about it never fully goes away. Our perspectives on sex and sexuality are skewed by imaginary expectations based on boasts, movies, porn, and maybe whatever we've heard women say about *Fifty Shades of Grey.* All that much more reason to learn and talk about sex in real terms— and to be sure to teach our kids about it as well.

To that end, you're about to meet two members of the Sex Wealthy, a couple who astounded me.

Meet the Sex Wealthy

I might not have believed this husband and wife existed if I hadn't interviewed them. Ever since, I've thought of them as the Sex McSexersons.

They have three young children including a baby and still manage to have sex several nights a week. Every week. "It's frequent and enjoyable," says Ryan Miller. "When we got married, we went into it saying, 'We're in this for the long haul.' We've never not had a good sex life."

When I picked my jaw up off the floor, I told Ryan I had to interview him and his wife, Sarah. So they took a break from their sexually utopian alternate universe to sit down and share their story.

"Our relationship is our top priority," Sarah said. "It's worth scheduling time for, even if we're exhausted." That's easy to say, but hard for most couples to actually do. But this couple's background gave them a unique perspective on sex. "My mom was a sex ed teacher. She was a childbirth educator and a doula. I held a flashlight and a mirror when my brother was born. I was four. It was not the first birth I had attended. I had been going to births my whole little life."

"In middle-school sex ed when we had to watch a video that included childbirth, our entire class screamed," I told her. "Literally— all of us."

"If you knew about that from a young age, you wouldn't have screamed," Sarah said.

Sarah and Ryan got to know each other when they acted out skits for her mother's classes. "I'd pretend I was pressuring her to have sex with me," Ryan says. All that time spent in multiple sex ed classes helped give him a realistic understanding at an early age as well.

"Maybe that's the difference for us," says Sarah. "We weren't exposed to all that fiction. There wasn't this big mystery surrounding it. We're very realistic about it."

There's also something else that makes Ryan extremely unusual. He doesn't masturbate, and says he never did.

At first, I didn't believe him. "Yeah, right, none of us do," I said, thinking he was joking.

"No, really."

"You never do anything by yourself?"

"No. It's been so long, it's like, why break the streak? I mean, I could if I wanted to. It never appealed to me. I had wet dreams, but never actively chose to. We're, like, so atypical."

Ryan says in his youth he was pushed against it by religious teachings. "I was always a rule follower, raised Lutheran. I didn't drink until I was twenty-one. I still am pretty rule-followy." He doesn't oppose masturbation now and says he has no problem with anyone else doing it. Sarah says she doesn't masturbate either. Both think that helps their sex life—they store it up for each other.

There is a price, they tell me. They don't get as much quiet time together as they'd like just to hang out. This is how they use much of their together time.

"I'll call her and tell her I'm thinking of her, or she'll text me saying she can't wait for me to come home," Ryan says. Knowing what's coming helps them enforce their kids' bedtimes too. The kids are down by 7:30. Ryan and Sarah move on to their own bed soon after.

"When we don't schedule it, I'll get home and be like, 'It's been so long!' And she'll say, 'It's been four days.'"

"Biologically, it's kind of a use-or-lose-it thing," Sarah says. "For women, if you stop having sex, it's easier to just keep not having sex."

Their sexual experiences aren't always intercourse. And sometimes, "I'm just, 'Can we just fuck and get it over with?'" Sarah says. Their jaunts can last anywhere from five minutes to two hours.

"It sounds easy in this conversation, but it's work," Ryan says. "I work full-time, she works part-time, and her schedule is constantly changing." Sarah works with children who have special needs. She's also a doula and lactation educator.

During Sarah's first pregnancy, Ryan worried he would no longer be her "favorite person." But the two pulled through on their commitment to make each other number one. "We know parents who are, like, 'The children have to be the priority,'" Ryan says. "We love them so much. But she's the first person I kiss when I come home. And I make sure they know that."

I told Sarah and Ryan about a great line my wife has for this: "The kids need to know that you and I are number one to each other and that they're number one to us."

I asked Ryan what he thinks the most important things are for people, particularly guys, to learn that we weren't taught.

"That it's not about them. It's about two people. It's about a way to build a relationship and not just a way to feel good. Sometimes it's just a back rub that can lead anywhere, or nowhere. There's no Judy Blume for guys. No young adult novels for guys in junior high, like about your first wet dream and so on. We need anything that promotes the conversations."

"Boys need a rite of passage," Sarah says. "Girls start their period; now you're a woman, you can procreate. There's nothing for boys."

"Boys hide magazines under the bed, the tissues, the underwear. It's embarrassment, it's shame," Ryan says. "The guys who are talking about it are bragging. It's unrealistic. How can you communicate about sick kids and the need for time off from work if you can't communicate at the start? Boys don't have anyone telling them what's healthy."

Are we teaching our kids what's healthy? Not just in sex, but in life? Are we setting good examples, demonstrating the healthiest ways to live? This leads us to the final section of this book—a look at how we can, and should, be sure to take care of ourselves in this all-in parenting life.

PART VI

The All-In Life

Body

O n a scale from one to ten, in which one is a pencil point and
ten is the love child of Stretch Armstrong and Elastigirl,
how stretched out do you feel?"

That's a question I asked many of the dads interviewed. I call it the
Stretched Out Scale. And, to no surprise, most responded with high
numbers. "Eight at this point," said Robert Loftus, who is helping build
the Great Dads Society, a support group for fathers. He is "beyond
busy" as a stay-at-home father, but emphasizes that it's his choice. "I
love being at home raising the kids, so I wouldn't change it for anything
in the world." The biggest problem, he says, is how little sleep he gets.
That's what pretty much all the great dads I interviewed said.

"We need to work on the frenetic lifestyle of America and how we
care for parents, support and uplift them, especially those who are
struggling," said Charlie Capen, the Hollywood actor, social media
manager for Netflix, and cocreator of the largely humorous website
HowToBeADad.com. "I don't sleep. I don't know if it's a side effect of
wanting to provide for my sons. I can be reached by e-mail and text at
any time; there's the expectation that you're always available. There's
this churn happening, and if you step away from the churn at any
time, it's like, 'What's wrong with you?'"

My oldest child helped me see this lack-of-sleep problem in America in a new light. When he was three years old, for a few weeks he suddenly began misbehaving. He was always a wonderful kid, and we had never had those problems. His preschool teachers noticed the change as well.

I called his doctor. "The first thing to check," she told me, "is the amount of sleep he's getting." That was a "Eureka!" moment. He had been fighting us about going to bed at night. I thought that was just his way of being stubborn or a symptom of whatever was making him act up in general. It wasn't—it was the cause. That night I began strictly enforcing bedtime. Within two days, he was behaving well again. One of his teachers said to me, with a big smile, "He's back!"

Our need for sleep doesn't end at youth. Imagine how much better, nicer, more courteous, and more respectful we could all be if we got enough sleep. I'm convinced there would be fewer fights and divorces, for starters. And imagine what our country could achieve. "Insufficient sleep is a public-health epidemic," the Centers for Disease Control and Prevention says. It's "linked to motor vehicle crashes, industrial disasters, and medical and other occupational errors."[1]

More than three in ten Americans aren't getting the recommended seven hours a night. Some of those are parents of young children.[2] Even many parents who get the total number of recommended hours have the problem of interrupted sleep. If your kids or your worries wake you up and you rarely finish a complete cycle, you can even be exhausted after having been in bed for nine hours.

So we caffeinate. For me, it's one sugar-free Red Bull each workday. I like to say that "I sip it like an IV drip." It takes me eight hours to finish. It's not ideal, but my doctor's fine with it, and I hate coffee.

I try to regiment a healthy lifestyle, partly through working out with trainers three times a week. That's the only thing I do regularly that isn't for work or my family. Then again, I often bring the two boys to the gym too. What I don't do enough of, perhaps ironically given how much I like this phrase, is stretch out. Sitting in one place long enough to do a series of stretches is an uphill battle for me. But I'm starting to do better.

There is something else I try to do, which took years to learn. When I'm hungry, I try to sit down and eat. Unless it's dinner time, when we sit together, there's a constant need for things to be done. My kids want me to play with them, make them snacks, get them things they can't reach, take them out. I joke that my boys have two modes at home: attack Daddy and screen time. And since we generally limit screen time to one hour a day (with screen-free Saturdays), it's a lot of attack Daddy. I've got my household chores too. But if I decide that I'll eat "when I have a free moment," I won't. So I announce "I'm not available," sit down, and try to spend five continuous minutes eating.

In modern parenthood, taking care of your own body is difficult. You have to force it. But it can be done. "It's about making a commitment and keeping it," says Dai Manuel, dad of two, personal trainer, and fitness blogger. He's one of those ridiculously muscular guys you see on magazine covers—literally. He's been on several.

"It's easy to put health on the back burner. But, you know, twelve to thirty-six months down the road, the little things you don't do anymore, and suddenly you're twenty pounds overweight, you've got high cholesterol and other problems. So keep the commitment."

Dai is part of a burgeoning industry focusing on dad fitness. "Give me fifteen minutes a day. I can work with that," he says. He lives in Canada, but many of his online followers are in the United States, and he travels in the States speaking at events.

"The hardest part is starting, getting yourself up and off that couch—that initial hour of inertia to get your butt, which is at rest, moving. But once you get up and move around, and feel the benefits and endorphins, and sleep better, and handle stress better, things begin to click. That's when it gets easy. When I say 'easy,' I mean it becomes a lifestyle, and you enjoy doing it."

But there's also a dark side to the fitness industry. Movies and magazine covers showing ridiculously massive models with exploding pecs and washboard abs can skew men's perceptions of what healthy looks like, just as women can be affected by covers of beauty magazines. "Manorexia" and muscle dysmorphia, also known as the Adonis Complex, show that men can become just as obsessive about their bodies.

"There are some images that create the false idea that that's what we have to do to be fit," Dai says. "I can tell you honestly, based on personal experience and friends in that industry, those models are some of the most unhealthy people. To get photo-ready, they go through diuretics, calorie reduction. I have friends who do bodybuilding, and to get ready for a show they are miserable people—especially when they're on calorie restrictions; they get depleted."

Dai encourages dads to focus not primarily on vanity, but on lifestyle. "What do you want to do five years from now, ten years from now, twenty years from now, from a physical standpoint? When I talk about the long-term goal, that's where it cements itself more for dads."

For this book, I wanted to find out how the health of today's parents compares to that of adults without children or parents of previous generations. I was astounded to find that our country doesn't have that information. I bugged the folks at the National Center for Health Statistics, the National Library of Medicine, and the CDC. Nada. We spend billions of dollars on scientific research and carry out a huge number of studies and surveys every year. But nothing has looked specifically at the overall health of parents. We should. Seeing how well or how poorly we're doing in our all-in lives could give us a serious wake-up call.

There have been some small studies with very specific findings on parental health, like that dads gain weight during their wives' pregnancies[3] and after the child is born.[4] One study found that parents with one or two kids may be less likely to get colds than their childless counterparts, but it didn't find out why.[5] Another found that married men without kids have a higher risk of dying from heart disease after age fifty than men with two or more kids.[6] But that doesn't mean parenthood is keeping us alive. It's possible that the same physical factors that gave these men the "reproductive fitness" to have multiple children also gave them better cardiovascular health.

Our bodies can respond in very different ways to this all-in lifestyle. Here are five steps we can take to protect our health, but the first is by far the most important:

1. *See your doctor.* Yes, you can find the time. Learn how every part of you is doing, and whether the pace of modern parental life is taking a physical toll.

2. *Make self-care a priority.* Get exercise. Insist on some relaxation time. Sleep at night. It's as important as taking care of your child. Michelle Azriel, mom of a three-year-old girl, puts this brilliantly: "You put the oxygen mask on yourself first. I'm still learning that. You have to take care of yourself."

3. *Sit down to eat.* Among the many benefits is the fact that you will realize what you're putting into your body and just how healthy or unhealthy that fuel is. This one decision has made a big difference for me.

4. *Know your why.* When parents build healthier lives, Dai Manuel says, it's because they've figured out their motivation. "My kids are the reason for keeping a healthy lifestyle. So I can be a better dad. When they have kids, I want to be a fit granddad, not having to worry about my health. So thirty minutes a day—that's me time."

5. *Have realistic goals.* Don't aim to look like people on those magazine covers I mentioned. That's not what people look like, and many of those people aren't healthy. Aim for how you want to feel and how much energy you want to have, Dai says.

Of course, as parents we're lucky in this respect too. One of the most relaxing, healthy experiences is to tune everything else out and just have fun being with your family.

My friend Jim, a dad whose kids are grown, says my baby daughter is the best "cardiovascular medicine," because "holding her is the most calming thing in the world." He's right. When I cuddle up with one of my kids or play ball with them, if I allow myself to get lost in the moment, I feel an incredible calm. A study at the University of Houston found that the more a man is involved with his family, the better his own mental health and well-being are.[7]

Still, sometimes parents feel crushed by the stress. I did once. A girl who was shot in the jaw helped set me straight.

Mind

I stood by my wife's side of the bed in the middle of the night. She was fast asleep. I reached down and tapped her arm a few times to wake her up.

"I'm doing well, right? I've made good decisions, right? It's—it's all okay?"

She had never seen me like this. We met shortly after college, and I've always been the one who sleeps like a baby. We joke about the fact that even seconds after I say, "Good night," she can't talk, because she'll wake me up. But on this night, in 2012, my mind was spiraling.

If I had known more about mental health, I could have seen it coming. For a month leading up to that night, I had been popping an over-the-counter sleep medication just about every night. My days were incredibly busy—literally nonstop, just like those of so many other parents. When I got in bed to crash and get five or maybe six hours of sleep, I had a sinking feeling that stress and worries might get the best of me. The pill let me avoid it. But on this night, that pill didn't work. So I panicked.

"Will I be able to sleep again?" I asked her.

"Of course," she said. "You just need to calm down. You're doing great. Everything's going to be fine. And you have to call Joe." Joe is my therapist. I call him that even though I go for years without seeing him, and when I do it's usually just two or three times.

But it was the middle of the night. So I decided to go downstairs and turn on the TV. A mass shooting had just taken place at a movie theater in Aurora, Colorado. Another American horror. I had the next day off from work, but volunteered to come in and help cover the story. Before the day was over, the network had asked me to go cover it. I was booked on a flight for the next morning.

That night, I called my doctor. "You really don't know what this is you're experiencing?" he asked.

"No."

"It's anxiety. It's very common. You've made it to this point in your life without really experiencing it."

I was always pretty stress-free. In high school, friends would ask why I seemed so relaxed when we had so much work to do and such busy schedules. I'd say, "Why worry? I know that when I wake up all my homework will be done and ready to hand in." I meant that I knew I'd get my work done, so why worry? But my friends joked that I had gremlins who did the work for me while I slept. When they felt stressed and I didn't, they'd ask to borrow my gremlins.

It was similar in college. People used to ask why I was always so cheerful, even during finals. I just always knew that things would work out. After graduation, when I moved to Atlanta with no job and nothing but a dream of becoming a broadcaster, I knew it would happen.

But parenthood changes that. Responsibility for the lives of your little kids, who look to you for everything, is a whole different kind of pressure. Having faith that everything will work out was no longer enough. "This *is* the future," I told myself. I felt that I needed to do better all around—make more money, spend more time with the kids, take us on more vacations. Working in a tumultuous, unstable field that can boost your ego one day and crush it the next probably didn't help matters.

But there was also more bothering me—I was concerned about

the state of the world. I want it to be better for my kids. I'm in an extremely unusual line of work, even among journalists. Every day I take part in covering the world's top stories. This often means the worst of humanity—bombings, wars, mass shootings, instability. Not to mention natural disasters. These things get to me on a very personal level.

Joe once asked me, "Which is more real to you—the typical parenting stresses or the fighting in Syria?" He thought the answer would be easy.

"Both," I told him. "Every time I swipe my credit card at the gas station, I count the number of steps between my bank and terrorist groups." (It's not that many.)

I don't accept what's wrong in the world. I have a fire in me to try to do something about it. That's good and bad. Fighting the good fight matters, but accepting things you can't control is necessary for mental health. Joe has told me several times that, just like most people, I wrestle with that acceptance. He says it hit me deeply. "You've never really stopped to deal with the traumatic things you've been through," he says, including my first son's heart surgery and my second son's birth.

On the night that I freaked out in 2012, it was all hitting me. So before hopping on the flight to Colorado, I went to see Joe. "What happened last night was that my mind and body got together to tell me, 'Enough is enough. You have to stop running away from your worries and deal with them,' " I told him. He gave me a book with some mental exercises.

To me, that was exciting. I love having things to work on, to attempt to fix.

As I guess you already know from this book, I'm happy to dive in head first when I see something needs to be done. So I committed to work on it.

After packing my suitcase for the flight to Denver, I did one more thing that people—especially men—don't often talk about publicly. I went to the pharmacy to pick up a prescription my doctor had called in for anti-anxiety medication. I felt good about the idea of having that for the trip and the coming days. It was about a two-week supply. It was like using crutches after breaking your leg.

On the flight, I started thinking about trauma counselors who travel around to mass shootings in America to help people in the aftermath. How do they handle all that, seeing horror after horror? After landing, I went and interviewed some for a story. They taught me about "vicarious trauma," and how they "check in" with themselves and each other to assess mental state.

Obviously the most important thing about that trip was covering the story. I interviewed the brother of one of the girls who was killed. It was heartbreaking. And I'll never forget my interview with McKayla Hicks, a teenager who was shot in the jaw.

"It changed me as a person," she told me. "I just don't take people for granted—especially the ones that save your life. Being in a real life-or-death situation," she said, helped her realize that "the little things don't matter. It shows you what really does matter."

"I think it's cool that I have a bullet in my chin," she added, calling it "a souvenir."[1] Her courage, resilience, and perspective were inspirational.

Two days after leaving Colorado, I was in Chicago giving a speech, called "Shine," to hundreds of teens at a convention for HOBY, the Hugh O'Bryan Youth Leadership Foundation. I told them how incredible it was to be there to take in their positivity and energy. It reminded me of the hope and optimism I usually feel and helped reignite them.

When I got back to Atlanta, I saw Joe once a week for several weeks. I'm sure I should see him more often than I do. Still, fortunately, I haven't had that problem again. And now I know the warning signs.

I share all this because, even in this new era, men still don't open up enough about mental health. We need to. It's part of all our lives.

After I mentioned my therapist in a speech, several guys shared their experiences with me. Carter Gaddis told me he's in therapy. "The reason I mention it is that you did," he said. Carter got laid off the year of the financial collapse, 2008. Within a year he had a heart attack and had a stent put in. He's healthy, but doesn't exercise as he should, he told me.

"I think the stress definitely weighs on us heavily, often," said his wife, Beth.

In therapy, Carter said, he works on "finding a way to juggle everything, to get on a career path that is gratifying for me and helps support our family."

Some dads, like my friend Aaron, whom I mentioned earlier, say they've had periods of using alcohol as medication. Josh Azriel said that during the first year of his daughter's life, he began drinking rum every night.

"It was really just a thimbleful, maybe two," his wife, Michelle, said.

"It was also wine," Josh responded. "I didn't tell you how frequently I was drinking. Just to sort of take the edge off."

He was at ten on the Stretched Out Scale, he says. "I didn't really enjoy coming home. Work for me was salvation."

"He not only came home, giving me a break and help," Michelle said, "but he was shouldering the burden of a lot of the issues I was having as well. And because I didn't have that network of moms in the beginning and I had Josh, I put everything on him."

Josh says he could have used "a dad support group that helped me learn how to help my wife, so I would have known what we needed. It would be great if a hospital, doctor's office, or church group did this, and checked up on you."

John Kinnear, father of two in Salt Lake City, wants hospitals to offer programs for men when their babies are born. "As a dad in the hospital, I was completely useless. There were so many dads on my floor whom I got to know because we were going to get food and walking like zombies. All these dads in sweatpants and T-shirts wandering the halls—it seriously looked like *Night of the Living Dead.*"

"That would be a perfect time to gather dads and offer classes about how to help your wife and child," and keep your own sanity, John says. "We took some classes beforehand, but they were with pillows and dolls. Hospitals should have programs involving the fathers right then."

Although Josh's daughter is adopted, he thinks a similar program, whether in a hospital or elsewhere, could have helped him understand what Michelle would be going through and how he could best support her without running himself ragged. These days, on the Stretched Out Scale he's gone from a ten down to an eight. "If I've had a tough day at work and come home and we have behavioral issues, that's when it gets tough on me. I've also learned that my eye will try to twitch slightly when I'm overly stressed or overly tired, and that's become a sign for me now."

He's found an escape. "I've gotten addicted to an online game, Clash of Clans. It's ridiculous, but it's a way to turn my brain off."

"I know the feeling," I told him. I don't play video games, but I have word-game apps and Sudoku on my phone, which I love to delve into. For those minutes, it feels as though I'm crawling into a separate space purely for myself. It's a virtual escape from endless responsibilities.

Some dads go much farther in the search for inner peace. Julian Redwood's path began in his younger days. It included "thousands of hours sitting with my eyes closed, listening to people who had been doing it a lot longer than me," including at a retreat in India and a meditation center in northern California. "I was going to become a Buddhist monk for a while," he says.

Now a marriage and family therapist, he works with dads to help them find peace. "I try to help all my clients turn toward the discomfort," to face what's bothering them, he says.

Some dads face a far bigger struggle: mental illness. One woman is helping lead the charge on that front because of a tragedy in her family.

"He was a very successful businessman, thirty-four, very charismatic," Sally Spencer-Thomas says of her brother, Carson Spencer. He was diagnosed with bipolar disorder at nineteen and, as the years went by, did not get all the help he needed. "In the summer of 2004, he had a full-blown episode of mania, and turned his life into a train wreck. He left his wife and daughter, spent all his money. When he came down from that, he couldn't recover. He denied being acutely suicidal, and said he'd never do it because of his daughter. I was a psychologist, and that was good enough for me. But he was a tortured soul."

The week before he committed suicide, Carson told Sally that he would get through it, "but it's madness." His use of that term makes Sally think what worried Carson most was the stigma. "He had a hard time reconciling being a 'man's man' with mental illness."

In his memory, Sally and others started Man Therapy, a nonprofit aimed at getting men and the women who love them the help they need.[2] "We discovered that white, working men with diagnosable diseases are the majority among suicides," Sally says. "Men receive tons of messages from the time they're little: don't ask for help, don't show weakness, don't be the weak link on the team. It builds resiliency, but when illness happens, that's something you can't really control."

Her organization uses humor to get its message out. Man Therapy created an online character called Dr. Rich Mahogany, who says things like, "Man Therapy is so manly, it'll put hairs on your brain."

"He's like Ron Burgundy," the character played by Will Ferrell in the *Anchorman* movies, Sally says. At the website, an actor sits before a background image of an office with a buck's head smack in the middle of the wall. "Don't bullshit me—there's nothing I hate more than bullshit, except maybe shopping malls," he says in one of the videos that pops up. He also explains that opening up about your feelings is "one of the least unmanly things" a guy can do.

The site includes videos from real men who describe their own experiences. One, identified as Zach, says that after his divorce, "It all kind of came crashing down." He had what he later figured out was a panic attack. "I've broken bones on the football field and torn ligaments on a basketball court, but none of that prepared me for that moment."

Zach began to feel his life didn't matter, just like a lot of men who are "literally or figuratively dying inside," he says. But he wanted to get better for his kids. Therapy helped because "over time, you really start to realize that the more you share, the more you can really start to heal from it. We need each other. That's how we're built. We're built for community."

We grow up in groups, from preschool through college, Zach says. "But then the rest of our lives we're supposed to be these fiercely independent lone wolves proving to ourselves and the rest of the world how we can do it alone." He calls it the "machismo route" and says, "You have to get past that."

A recent study warned against the dangers of assuming that men are okay after a divorce. "Researchers now report that divorced men have higher rates of mortality, substance abuse, depression, and lack of social support," *PsychCentral* reported.[3]

Men are "affected substantially by psychological trauma and negative life events," Dr. Ridwan Shabsigh, of Cornell University Medical School, said in the article. He added, "Research is urgently needed to investigate the prevalence and impact of such effects and to develop diagnosis and treatment guidelines for practitioners."

If any dad suffering from anxiety, stress, or mental illness wonders whether there really is a community that will support him, he need only look at Lorne Jaffe, who stood before hundreds of fellow fathers and read from his blog about his struggles. "I didn't think I was ready for this. My therapist, my best friend, my wife said, 'This is an opportunity; you have to do this," Lorne told me after the event at the Dad 2.0 Summit. "I didn't sleep the night before."

His courage was rewarded. After Lorne spoke, the crowd erupted in a standing ovation. "I don't understand when people are appreciative and complimentary," he said in our interview. "I don't understand validation."

Lorne suffers from extreme anxiety and depression. He's in good company—more than 6 million men suffer from depression each year.[4] In Lorne's case, it's something he's battled since childhood. He says it was brought on, at least in part, by his father. "He was very hard on me and sarcastic. He stopped showing me physical affection at four and favored my sister." At age eleven, Lorne developed gynecomastia, swelling of the breast tissue. He says his parents didn't get him any help. "I spent my life hiding." He finally got an operation at twenty-nine.

As an adult, Lorne has had breakdowns. Now a married stay-at-home dad on disability, he blogs about his adventures at Raising Sienna.com. Being a father has made him want to get better. What he wants most is to empower his daughter with the confidence he never had. "I will support my daughter in whatever she wants to do. I will never pressure her. I will direct and guide. I don't want her to be scared like me. I don't want her to be me. I want her to have a happy life and feel loved. I want her to know she can come to me and come to her mom, even if it's just for a friggin' hug."

Mental-health problems can come in many forms, from stress to depression to a severe disorder. Here are some helpful resources everyone should check out, either for yourself or for a man in your life. Some of these are also helpful in seeking ways to improve physical health:

National Institute of Mental Health (nimh.nih.gov): This
government agency has information and publications on men's
mental health, fact sheets on stress, anxiety, and depression, and
a lot more.
American Psychiatric Association (psychiatry.org): This site talks
you through the symptoms and warning signs of depression,
specifically in men.
Man Therapy (mantherapy.org): As I mentioned, this site uses
humor to goad guys into getting the help they need. Among

the main features is a massive alphabetical list of healthy ways
to cope with anger and stress, from "adopt a dog" to "zombie
crawl."

WebMD (webmd.com/men/guide): A section on anger
management offers advice including "deep breathing," "positive
self-talk," and communication exercises.

Centers for Disease Control and Prevention (cdc.gov/men/az/
mentalhealth.htm): The CDC has extensive research that may
help with mental and physical health concerns.

Office on Women's Health (womenshealth.gov/mens-health/mental-
health-for-men): The fact that the U.S. government has this office
but no similar one for men speaks to other issues we've discussed
in this book. (There's also a girlshealth.gov, but no boyshealth.gov.)
Still, it does at least have a section on men's health. The website
offers information on physical and mental health as well as "violence
prevention"—aiming to help both abusers and the abused. "Men
are sometimes victims of intimate partner violence (also known
as domestic violence)," it notes. "Men may feel uncomfortable
reporting it. But if you have been attacked, remember that you
are not at fault, and you do not deserve to be hurt."

Some dads say they find the confidence, healing, and calm they
need by focusing on the third part of who they are.

Spirit

Y ou've got to be really intentional about it," Jim Daly told me. I had asked for his thoughts, as president and CEO of the Christian ministry Focus on the Family, about how today's parents can find spiritual peace. "Find ways to do family devotions— for us it's just reading together," he said. "We take twenty minutes; we don't overdo it."

Jim sits down for this ritual with his wife and two boys, thirteen and eleven, every night. "We share it. We get a little math in there. We'll say, 'This chapter in Matthew is forty verses, so how much is that each? Then we each read and do a quick little chat. Their attention spans aren't too long, so you gotta be respectful of that, but it's been great."

Activities like this can work for families of any religion, he said. It helps instill a calm in daily life. And it's time "that you can connect as a family to transmit values, to have fun, to laugh, to just be together in a healthy context. You're not going after them for doing homework, you're not going after them for something they didn't do, the chores, or whatever. It's just a more relaxed and relational time. Your kids draw closer to you."

When I told Jim I was reaching out to people of various religions to discuss how parents can find spiritual peace—whatever that means to them—in the hectic American lifestyle, he was excited. Spiritual peace isn't just something he pursues within his family. It saved him after a childhood of fatherlessness.

"I was an orphan kid, I lived in foster care. I didn't have a dad. I had four dads, though technically three. I had an alcoholic father; a stepfather who abandoned the family the day of my mother's funeral when I was nine; a foster father who accused me of trying to murder him when I was nine and a half; and my biological father, who came back into my life and then died when I was twelve."

"Do you remember being a kid and just wishing that you had a good dad who was there for you?" I asked.

"Yeah, every day. I played quarterback in high school. Every season, we had dad's night, and every season nobody came out on the field for me." The school offered to have another dad come out for him. And once, his older brother, who was at that point his legal guardian, stepped out for him. But the other years Jim didn't want anyone to. "I said, 'No, that's fine.' It didn't hurt me that night. The pain of it was that it was the evidence of what I lacked."

At fifteen, Jim became Christian. "Did God provide you the father figure that you didn't have in humanity?" I asked.

"Absolutely. Absolutely."

Still, the pain doesn't go away. Jim describes a time not long ago when he just wished he had a dad he could call. "And you know, in my heart, God said to me, 'Haven't I been a good father to you?' And I just went flat on my face. I said, 'You've been an awesome dad.' And I think at the core, that's who we need to be first. Just, loving and kind, vulnerable, knowing our imperfections, and willing to embrace those around us who aren't perfect." Having that daily family ritual helps him be all those things, Jim says.

Pastor Ed Young calls it "quiet time with the Lord." As the leader of one of the nation's largest congregations—the sprawling Second Baptist Church of Houston—he makes it a morning ritual, which he compares to brushing his teeth. "I have a very structured routine in the morning that I have been committed to for years. It includes prayer, scripture reading, and two cups of coffee. The structure of it provides a framework on which I can depend when life is chaotic, as it often is. It is rare that I alter or ignore the regimen, even down to the coffee I make. That discipline has served me well in times of heartache, joy, peace, and chaos."

And the Sabbath is essential, says Young, who has three children and eleven grandchildren. "The Lord commanded a Sabbath for a reason. Orthodox Jews have set the bar for the standard. To them, the Sabbath is a way of life not based on convenience or capriciousness. The Sabbath is sacred. The Sabbath is family. The Sabbath is restorative."

Michael Kress celebrates the Jewish Shabbat, from sundown on Friday to sundown on Saturday. "That's been extraordinarily valuable to us as a family. No screens, no phones. It's been incredible. We generally go to services. Presence is extremely hard in society now. Shabbat is forced time. It's enforcing a certain amount of presence."

I'm Jewish as well and once gave a sermon explaining that I keep kosher because it serves as a reminder, every time I eat, of the history that led to today. It gives me perspective and helps remind me to care for my spirit.

David Wolpe, who was named America's "top rabbi" by *Newsweek*, has had particularly acute challenges in his life. Sure, he's busy, as head of Temple Sinai in Los Angeles, one of the biggest Conservative congregations in the country. But he and his wife are also both cancer survivors. They've raised a daughter, who wrote in *The Huffington Post* about what a "great man" and "great dad" David is.[1]

David has spoken out about how prayer helped him find peace. "It's important for everyone to have their own spiritual practice," he says.

I asked what "spiritual peace" means to him.

"It's a place of refuge that you can go to. You don't stay there all the time—at least I don't. But you know that for that half hour in the morning when you're praying or whatever it is that you do, that you have a sanctuary from the noise and obligations that continually press upon you in the world and the worries that crowd your mind. Your spiritual practice acts as a protected space into which you can go."

David prayed every day during his battle with cancer. "Not because I expected a result, like God would come down and say, 'Okay, you prayed. I'm going to cure your cancer.' I prayed for refuge."

"That was the result," I said. "You found spiritual peace amid the battle."

"Exactly. When you enter that spiritual place, you're understanding that ultimately whatever happens, you're able to accept."

"So if you find that you're getting caught up in worries and stresses, is that a sign that you need to do some kind of spiritual practice?"

"I think it's definitely an indicator that it would be helpful to do whatever your refuge is. No one can sustain the constant assault of the world all the time. It's not healthy. It's not good. And it stunts your emotional growth."

Parents, more than ever, need to teach kids this, David says. For example, "Getting into college is a much, much more difficult and expectation-laden process than it was when I did it. There's just a lot of pressure."

"Does that need to change?"

"That's a big question in social policy," David says. But the way things are now, "It's a lot of pressure—too much."

He cited a line from Deuteronomy: "Guard your soul carefully."

"We need to begin with the acknowledgment that each person has a deeper self that needs cultivation and care. If we don't take ourselves seriously, then we will not be able to serve as mentors and models to our children. You can't be the steward of another soul and remain neglectful of your own."

Taking the time to find spiritual peace can help men be the fathers they need to be, David says. "A real man has a sympathetic eye and a sincere heart. Aim for these and those who love you will be blessed."

"Can a feeling of spiritual peace stay with you during the rest of your day?" I asked.

"Sometimes. Sometimes you just lose it. My guess is the most sedate guru in the world doesn't like it when he gets a flat tire! I just don't think people are built that way."

Tushar Tank might not claim that mantle, but he is a devout Hindu who was recommended to me by the leadership of BAPS (Bochasanwasi Shri Akshar Purushottam Swaminarayan Sanstha), the spiritual organization behind huge, gorgeous Hindu temples sprouting up in the United States and around the world. Tushar cites the teaching: "To enhance peace in the world, we must first engender peace in our communities, which in turn requires that we create peace within our families. That ultimately means we need to change ourselves and create peace within our own spirits. Children are great actors. They will become what they see."

Meditation is key. "We try to quiet our minds and focus our thoughts on our guru and God. This helps us start our day in a positive way. As parents, being positive and quieting the mind help us start the day stress-free. Also our kids see us meditate every morning and this serves as a great example for them to also begin practicing."

Tushar, who has a seven-year-old daughter and a six-year-old son, also talked about Hindu food restrictions as a way of keeping that sense of spirit alive throughout the day. And he said something that inspired me to adopt a new ritual: "As fathers, a traditional part of our daily meditation is to apply the *tilak-chandlo,* a red sandalwood circle within a yellow *U* shape, to our foreheads. This is a symbol that reminds us to always be at the service of others. And it serves as a constant reminder to maintain our positive spirit throughout the day. Whenever you look in the mirror, you get a gentle nudge to stay grounded and not sweat the small stuff.

"One day I was trying to help my son with some simple addition, and he clearly had other ideas. I was getting anxious. All the worries of the day and thoughts about how this child will succeed in life without learning addition were starting to surface in this one interaction. However, when he mentioned that my *tilak-chandlo* was smudged, all this evaporated. In that moment I realized that I needed to be happy, and then he would be too. We never finished the addition problem, but we had a great evening. We read books about underpants instead."

"Symbols are powerful methods to remind us to stay grounded throughout our day," Tushar added, noting that some people of other religions do this by wearing symbols, and charity groups do it with their messaging through wristbands with words printed on them.

For weeks after he said this, I couldn't get the image out of my mind. I got online, created, and ordered a wristband that I now wear often. It says, "All In." It reminds me to fight the good fight for family life *and* to live to the fullest.

For Islamic scholar David Dakake, a professor at George Mason University, the Salat, a prayer ritual that takes place five times throughout the day, is the key. It is important for counteracting "forgetfulness" of core religious beliefs, he says. "I feel that the greatest gift I can give to my child is prayer. You can teach your child how to live in this world, how to do this or that, and yet for all the worldly teaching that we do as parents, that child is still subject to the vicissitudes and buffeting of this world.

"But to give your child a life of prayer is to give them a doorway to step outside the limitations and uncertainties of earthly life, a chance to 'become'—not just in this world, which as the Quran says is 'passing away like clouds,' but to become what we are in God's eyes, as God made us: a creature who worships Him.

"As parents there are many expectations and hopes that we have for our children: educational achievement, social acceptance, financial success, and so on. But the greatest pride that I have felt is in seeing my son, on his own, stand up and face Mecca, make the *adhan* [call to prayer], and bow in prayer."

The similarities among what all these religious leaders said emphasizes that we are all in this together. And these kinds of rituals, whether involving a religion or not, can help anyone achieve a break from the hamster wheel of modern parenting. It might be tough to find the time. But that's part of the problem. All these religious leader dads as well as numerous experts I've spoken with say there's a fundamental decision we can make as parents that will help us find this calm time without feeling guilty. It requires doing one simple thing.

The Value of Less

I t takes work to have children who are children," says Jeff Bogle, dad of two daughters in Exton, Pennsylvania. The pace of life today, he says, is pushing kids to grow up too soon.

"My big parenting decision is to elongate childhood, to leave that room accessible for as long as my kids want to be there. I feel there's a trend to rush kids through it, shoveling them into one adult-led activity after another and exposing them to sights, sounds, media, and commercialism that strip away the simple joy and innocence. You only get one shot at that. It seems some parents are like, 'I'm tired of that. I want a mini grown-up, and I don't know why.' It takes work to have children who are children. It's easier to let them lock themselves in the room watching TV and texting at age eight."

Millions of parents know what he means. We sign up our kids for numerous activities and, even if it doesn't seem like a lot, we quickly find ourselves turned into chauffeurs with just about enough time at home to eat dinner and collapse. "We overschedule and even compete about the level of 'busyness' our kids have," says Pastor Ed Young. "We are concerned about ADHD and learning challenges, yet we create and maintain a frenetic pace and chaotic environment for our kids."

A man I know was so fed up with this that he gave up a high-ranking job in global media to go live with his wife and daughter in a tiny village on a hilltop in southern Spain. "It's so tranquil," Tim Lister told me via Skype, because my publisher wouldn't foot the bill for my transatlantic visit with Tim, no matter how much I argued it was "necessary for reporting."

"It's great to be out of the rat race, to read and think more," said Tim, fifty-four. "I breathe fresh air and live among people who have a good work-life-family-rest balance. And being in the countryside, surrounded by nature, is really nice. There's more time here, and people aren't so consumed with rushing from A to B. They're not so preoccupied with making all the monthly payments you have when you're deep in the rat race. They don't have a great deal of income, but then they don't go out and spend a lot either. They have a lot of time on their hands. It's simple, straightforward, based on the land. And extended family is part of the scene here."

Try telling anyone about Tim and you'll see what I've seen: they daydream briefly about doing the same. Of course, most of us will never do anything this drastic. But some dads are finding ways to build less stretched-out lives for themselves and their families at home.

Jeff Funk, father of three, manages TV stations professionally. For fun, he pursues his passion. "I'm in a band with other guys. Four of the six of us have kids. I wanted to make sure that I could be happy, and music is a big part of who I am. We perform on Friday nights, and practice once, sometimes twice a week. My wife has her hobbies as well. My kids sometimes see me play, and the joy on their faces—I lose my concentration looking at them."

Seeing their dad spend time regularly doing something purely because he loves it sets a good example, Jeff says. It sends the message: Be yourselves. "We've got to let go of the reins a little bit. Just guide kids and nurture them. I grew up with a pretty strict mom. It forced me to be such a rebel; I don't want to repeat that."

Child psychologist Paula Bloom puts it this way: "Parents need to teach their kids to balance human doing with human being." Sometimes, she says, you just need to do nothing. That's easier said than done. We're so hyper-scheduled, how could our kids see us do nothing while they're awake? Also, it's tempting to keep our kids busy when we see other parents put their kids into all sorts of activities that those kids then excel at. But "as parents, we've got to get over our anxiety that we're not doing enough," Paula told me for a CNN.com column. "Creating a sense of safety, helping kids have confidence to try certain things—those are the things that matter."

One of my personal trainers, a great dad named Robert Stephens, agrees. He trains professional athletes, including NFL players and Olympians. He insists that kids should avoid organized sports until age eleven or twelve. Adults are "trying to instill grown-up values and a competitive nature in kids, who are nowhere near that yet," he says. "They're trying to make them into world champions. That's nuts!"[1]

Robert wants kids to start playing neighborhood pickup games again. "It teaches them how to regulate themselves, make up rules," and resolve situations, he says. Another big benefit to pickup games: parents can relax. We don't have to jump in and resolve everything. We don't have to set rules. The kids are better off, and so are we. Less really is more.

Unfortunately, pickup games are rare these days in many places, due to a cycle we need to break. Since so many kids get shepherded around to different adult-led activities, they're often not home for spontaneous play with each other. In our neighborhoods and the communities we build for ourselves, we can change that. The more we all cut back on the crazy schedules, the more we'll give our kids the space and freedom they need to play—and the more we'll give ourselves time to chill.

The best way to establish a lifestyle in which we don't feel the need to fuss over our kids every second is to start from the earliest days of their lives. Sometimes babies just want to lie still and look at a mobile or sit in a stroller and look around outside. But because so many of us parents have to go back to work just days after our kids come home, we want to use every second we have with them for interaction. The idea of just letting them chill while we chill is a foreign concept. To set the right pattern, we need real time together from the beginning.

"I don't understand why parents are not given more maternity and paternity leave," says Jeff Bogle, who runs the blog Out With The Kids. "I think that's where all change needs to come from." It's when families establish patterns that emphasize "forming bonds and making memories" over gadgets and distractions. "None of that happens if they're in day care."

He's right. Numerous studies find that routines established in the first months of life can have a huge impact on how the following years go for the entire family. With paid parental leave, parents have the freedom to work out a better, healthier lifestyle for their children and themselves.

See how everything comes full circle?

Loving Parenthood

Sure, parenthood has its tough moments. And there's a lot our society needs to do to make things better for the real modern family. But make no mistake, today's dads love parenthood. We want to make things better because we love it and want everyone else to have an even better, easier ride with it.

Having a child is like a Big Bang in your life. This whole new, amazing being is yours to care for. Just like moms, dads are now sharing their thoughts and advice on how to do your best and enjoy the journey. Writing *All In* has allowed me to meet fantastic fathers from all walks of life. Along the way, I've picked up pearls of wisdom:

Fatherhood brings me to my knees and empowers me in ways I never thought it would. I'm constantly bleeding out, but I'm the strongest I've ever been, because I'm impassioned by it.
—Charlie Capen

Ultimately, parenthood is an exercise in heartbreak, attaching yourself to these children you love more than anything. You do your job really well, and they will leave you forever. That's your goal: get them to a point where they will not need you.
—Jason Katims

I love it, man! It's crazy—on a genetic level, this is what I'm here for. My cells have told me that I should stay alive long enough to do this. My body is going, "This is good."
—Jay Ramsay

Parenthood has taught me to be more patient, to have a cool head in a time of crisis, to use common sense. And it's taught me to trust my gut, my instincts.
—Josh Azriel

A successful father listens to his kids. Kids want attention. So you've got to stop and not be distracted. Have a positive attitude. Assess your attitude. Be very supportive of your children. That doesn't mean not to discipline. Yeah, you're going to have to discipline. But after you discipline your children, make sure you hug them and love them. And make sure they understand why. That's how you be supportive. When there's difficulty, you have to execute a way to resolve situations. Take action. When your children are in trouble, respond.
—Rick Martin

I think the main thing is when they turn eighteen and they're ready to launch, I want them to be able, and know how, to love.
—Jim Daly

It's incredible. I know what I have and don't take it for granted, being in their lives.
—Whit Honea

Oren Miller, a stay-at-home dad in Baltimore, organized a Facebook page for dad bloggers like him to share thoughts every day, post questions, and ask for advice. A few months after I met him in 2014, he was diagnosed with stage IV lung cancer. He was forty-one, and

wrote a blog post about his diagnosis and love for parenthood. With
his permission, I'm sharing parts of it here:

In the summer of 2010, we were at Bethany Beach in Dela-
ware, and everyone was having a great time. Our family and
some friends were building sand castles, going in and out of the
water, and just relaxing in general—everyone except anxious
old me. I had hundreds of unread e-mails and dozens of ideas
for blog posts I didn't have time to write, and I was surrounded
by too much sand and not enough coffee. I tried to pretend I
was having a good time, but people could see I was out of my
comfort zone and, worse, that I didn't want to be there.

It was only on the drive back home that I had the epiphany. I
realized what I had been missing out on. It's the biggest tragedy
of human existence: I was having the time of my life and didn't
even know it.

That was a good day, since once you make that decision,
man, you're in heaven every single second of your life. Things
only got better, because I was able to repeat that decision
subconsciously from that moment on. It made the difference
between a living hell—where I was always behind, unhappy,
unfulfilled, a step behind in my writing and my relationships
with my wife, kids, and friends—and a living heaven, where
even if I had wanted more out of life, I also knew I had it all.

I believe in heaven on earth, and I believe it's found anywhere you seek it. I found heaven on long car rides with the
kids. I could have felt bad about having to drive my kids back
and forth to school for hours every day, but instead I used those
car trips to chat with my kids about their worlds and about
mine, to introduce them to music, and to make up music with
them, to talk about values as well as about nonsense.

I found heaven on the dirty floor of a basketball court. My
then two-year-old daughter used to finish preschool at noon, so

we were stuck for hours, waiting for her brother to finish school before we could head back home. And those days of waiting with my girl will be remembered forever by me and hopefully by her. For four hours, we sat around, shared lunch, went to a playroom at the JCC, where she made me plastic sandwiches and tea, and raced to the basketball court and played. She was leading a parade of two by stepping on the black line, and I was behind her, dribbling. She made up that game, calling it "going to the birthday party." Then we would sit down on the floor in front of each other, spread our legs, and roll the ball. She wanted to hug, so we hugged on the floor of the basketball court while people played around us.

Even heaven on earth includes some caveats. We recently moved to a beautiful dream house. It's where my kids will grow up, and it breaks my heart. I don't care about myself, I really don't. I've had the most amazing life anyone could ever wish to have. But there's one thing I would give anything for: watching my kids grow up.

I've raised happy kids. Sure, they sometimes whine, but in general, they're happy. They're my masterpiece: two loving, smart, intelligent, funny, happy kids. I can't let that end. I can't allow them to grow up sad. I can't allow them to grow up with a hole in their hearts in the shape of the dad they barely remember. I want them to be happy. I want to be around to make them happy. And I want my wife to be happy. She deserves to be happy. I wish I could make her happy right now.

So acceptance and sadness—well, I believe they can coexist. Sadness is inevitable. I'm only human, and trying too hard to rise above it only hurts more. But I do accept. I accept that life is finite, and I accept that my time will come soon. I accept that my life had been and still is a gift, and I accept the likely possibility that I won't see my kids grow older.

Should I complain, though? Should I cry out to the empty

sky and say, "Why me?" Or should I feel that now, even now, especially now, a little confused, a little tired, and a little sad, I'm having the time of my life?

Whatever happens to my body in the next few months is still relatively unknown. Here's what we do know, though: I'm the luckiest sonofabitch who's ever walked this earth. And we know I will be loved until my last moment by people it has been my utmost privilege to know: by a wife I adore and two kids I'm in awe of every single moment.[1]

Despite the horror that his life could be cut short, Oren knows he has been fortunate to have been home with his kids for these early years. His wife works for a private data company, and the family has been able to get by on her salary. As heartbreaking as his story is, imagine if Oren and his wife, like many couples, never got to make that choice.

Our laws, policies, and stigmas are standing in the way of our freedom—the freedom to design our lives in the ways that work best for our families and make us productive, satisfied workers. We're all paying a price for this—business owners, managers, moms, dads, and, most important, children. We can change this. We have to.

Let's Do This

Diagnosing problems is useless if you don't treat them. The problems we've looked at here, with experts and parents of such varied backgrounds weighing in, ail America. But as you've seen, we have the cures.

We can be the generation of parents that turns this around. We can demand the needed changes and make them happen. By following the steps laid out in this book, we can build a nation promoting "family values" that actually value families.

The fast-paced, active society we live in, placing numerous demands on us, is not going away. But how we handle it is our choice. We can give in to being tugged in multiple directions and try to grin and bear it. Or we can realize that we're all in this together, and summon our collective power to make changes. As a nation of parental Elastigirls and Stretch Armstrongs, we can use those arms to reach for things that were previously beyond our grasp—like new laws and policies, the high-hanging fruit of gender equality.

Men and women can lock arms, rise up, break down the structures boxing us in, and march forward together. To those women leading the battle, I hope this book has made absolutely clear to you that many, many men want to join you. Dads are invested in making these changes—and making them stick.

Parents generally don't feel like superheroes. But when our kids are little, they see us that way. They're right to. They see that we have the power to achieve incredible things. Let's use it, and be fueled every step of the way by the love we have for them.

Look out, America. Here we come.

Acknowledgments

Deep breath.

This is a space for me to acknowledge people whose work was vital in creating this book. But maybe you can use it also to reflect on those you wish to thank for helping you with something meaningful. I find that when I focus on appreciation, the world stops spinning so fast.

As for my list, here's how I think of it: Imagine pouring heart and soul into a project—a piece of art, a composition, anything. Now imagine it sitting in the depths of oblivion, unreachable. And now, imagine it not existing at all.

All these images come to mind because, yes, I've poured heart and soul into *All In*. But I'm acutely aware that it would be sitting in the depths of oblivion, or quite possibly wouldn't exist, if not for people who supported and, just as importantly, were willing to bet on me.

My terrific agent Mollie Glick set me on the right path: "This book is your call to action," she said. She shepherded it through the world of publishing and into the hands of the best team I could have asked for: HarperOne. Editors Roger Freet and Genoveva Llosa showed incredible passion for *All In,* and delivered. They are brilliant guides who made your reading experience better, as did production editor

Suzanne Quist. The entire HarperOne team—copy editors, designers, publicists, and more—are a joy to work with, and quite possibly rescued this book by getting rid of the more cerebral title I originally wanted and replacing it with the one it deserves. Thanks to Renee Senogles, Laina Adler, Mark Tauber, Claudia Boutote, and Terri Leonard. And to Adrian Morgan for the awesome cover.

Also thanks to my own stable of *All In* assistants, including C.S., Susanna, Leslie, Matt, Shaina, and D.J., for transcribing interviews, footnoting, fact checking, and being sources of encouragement. You rock.

That's the *All In* team. But my gratitude goes out to hundreds, even thousands of others. Early influencers who taught me to communicate and speak my mind, through example and instruction. Editors who made me a better reporter, especially in my early days at NPR and later days at CNN. Friends and colleagues who have been supportive during the tough and the joyful times.

And everyone who has fought for what's good and right, paving a path for my generation to have access to so much freedom and so many opportunities. *All In* is about delivering on my promise to you: to not take what we have for granted, and to keep pushing forward.

Finally, a giant thank-you to all the amazing, hardworking, committed dads and moms. If you're a parent, it's the most important role you'll ever have. Doing your best is a responsibility not just to your child, but to society. Guiding your children to appreciate and respect the gift of life is the ultimate success.

Notes

Introduction

1. Boris Groysberg and Robin Abrahams, "Manage Your Work, Manage Your Life," *Harvard Business Review,* March 2014.

2. Sheryl Sandberg, *Lean In: Women, Work, and the Will to Lead* (New York: Knopf, 2013).

3. Klaus Schwab, "Preface," in *The Global Gender Gap Report 2013* (Geneva: World Economic Forum, 2013), v.

4. Sheelah Kolhatkar, "U.S. to Working Parents: You're on Your Own," *Bloomberg Businessweek,* January 17, 2014, http://www.businessweek.com/articles/2014-01 -17/u-dot-s-dot-to-working-parents-youre-on-your-own.

5. Rebecca Traister, "The Uselessness of Hating Sheryl Sandberg," *New Republic,* February 27, 2014, http://www.newrepublic.com/article/116794/rosa-brooks-hates-sheryl-sandberg-and-misses-point.

6. Emma Watson, "Gender Equality Is Your Issue Too," *UN Women,* September 20, 2014, http://www.unwomen.org/en/news/stories/2014/9/emma-watson-gender-equality-is -your-issue-too (text of speech given at United Nations headquarters).

7. Gretchen Livingston, "Growing Number of Dads Home with the Kids: Biggest Increase Among Those Caring for Family," *Pew Research Center's Social and Demographic Trends,* June 5, 2014, 5.

8. National At-Home Dad Network, "Statistics on Stay-at-Home Dads," http:// athomedad.org/media-resources/statistics/.

9. United States Census Bureau, "One-Third of Fathers with Working Wives Regularly Care for Their Children, Census Bureau Reports," December 5, 2011, https:// www.census.gov/newsroom/releases/archives/children/cb11-198.html.

10. Kerstin Aumann, Ellen Galinsky, and Kenneth Mathos, "The New Male Mystique," *National Study of the Changing Workforce* (New York: Families and Work Institute, 2011), 2.

11. Brad Harrington, Fred Van Deusen, and Beth Humberd, "The New Dad: Caring, Committed, and Conflicted," Boston College, 2011, p. 16, http://www.bc.edu/content/dam/files/centers/cwf/pdf/FH-Study-Web-2.pdf.

12. Barack Obama, "We Need Fathers to Step Up," *Parade,* June 2011.

13. Rachel Weiner, "'Lonely' Obama Reaches Out to House GOP," *Washington Post,* January 14, 2013, http://www.washingtonpost.com/blogs/post-politics/wp/2013/01/14/obama-to-house-gop-come-over-play-cards/; Larry Hackett and Sandra Sobieraj Westfall, "The Obamas Talk to PEOPLE: 'Still a Lot of Work to Do,'" *People,* December 30, 2013, http://www.people.com/people/archive/article/0,,20771331,00.html.

14. Livingston, "Growing Number," 5.

15. Josh Levs, "Dads Reveal Struggle to Balance Work, Family," *CNN,* July 20, 2009, http://www.cnn.com/2009/LIVING/wayoflife/07/20/dads.and.recession/index.html.

16. Jason Ferrara, "Fewer Working Fathers Are Willing to Be Stay at Home Dads," *CareerBuilder,* June 6, 2009, http://www.careerbuilder.com/Article/CB-1283-The-Workplace-Fewer-Working-Fathers-are-Willing-to-Be-Stay-At-Home-Dads/.

17. Jeff Pearlman, "A Father's Day Wish: Dads, Wake the Hell Up!" *CNN,* June 17, 2011, http://www.cnn.com/2011/OPINION/06/16/pearlman.fathers.day/.

18. Kim Parker and Wendy Wang, "Modern Parenthood: Roles of Moms and Dads Converge as They Balance Work and Family," *Pew Research Center's Social and Demographic Trends,* March 14, 2013, 1.

19. Parker and Wang, "Modern Parenthood," 6.

20. Parker and Wang, "Modern Parenthood," 6.

21. Parker and Wang, "Modern Parenthood," 6.

22. Aumann, Galinsky, and Matos, "New Male Mystique," 5.

23. Jo Jones and William D. Mosher, "Fathers' Involvement with Their Children: United States, 2006–2010," *National Health Statistics Reports* 71 (2013): 6, http://www.cdc.gov/nchs/data/nhsr/nhsr071.pdf.

24. Ipsos Public Affairs, "As Father's Day Approaches, Dads of Young Children Say They Do Their Fair Share of Chores—Including Changing Diapers—But Moms Aren't So Sure," last modified June 10, 2010, http://www.ipsos-na.com/news-polls/pressrelease.aspx?id=4835.

25. Richard Dorment, "Why Men Still Can't Have It All," *Esquire,* June/July 2013, http://www.esquire.com/features/why-men-still-cant-have-it-all-0613.

26. Dorment, "Why Men Still Can't Have It All."

27. Dorment, "Why Men Still Can't Have It All."

28. Wendy Wang, "The 'Leisure Gap' Between Mothers and Fathers," *Fact Tank: News in the Numbers,* October 17, 2013, http://www.pewresearch.org/fact-tank/2013/10/17/the-leisure-gap-between-mothers-and-fathers/.

29. "American Time Use Survey," Bureau of Labor Statistics, http://www.bls.gov/tus/.

30. Terri Pous, "Women Lazier Than Men, Global Survey Finds," *Time,* July 22, 2012, http://newsfeed.time.com/2012/07/22/women-lazier-than-men-global-survey-finds/.

31. Pedro C. Hallal et al., "Global Physical Activity Levels: Surveillance Progress, Pitfalls, and Prospects," *Lancet* 380/9838 (July 2012): 247, doi:10.1016/S0140-6736(12)60646-1.

32. OECD Better Life Index, "Work-Life Balance." http://www.oecdbetterlifeindex.org/topics/work-life-balance.

33. "What About the Dads? Does Your Paternity Leave Policy Discriminate?" *National Law Review,* November, 2013.

34. Josh Levs, "Why I've Filed an EEOC Charge Against Time Warner," *levsnews,* October 30, 2013, http://joshlevs.tumblr.com/post/65567442495/why-ive-filed-an-eeoc-charge-against-time-warner.

35. Levs, "Why I've Filed."

36. Tara Siegel Bernard, "Standing Up for the Rights of New Fathers," *New York Times,* November 8, 2013, http://www.nytimes.com/2013/11/09/your-money/standing-up-for-the-rights-of-new-fathers.html.

37. "Male CNN Reporter Sues over Parental Leave Policy," *Today,* November 11, 2013, video, http://www.today.com/video/today/53520438#53520438.

38. Ben James, "New Dad's Bias Claim Puts Employers on Notice," *Law360,* November 1, 2013, http://www.law360.com/articles/485170/new-dad-s-bias-claim-puts-employers-on-notice.

39. Anna North, "Tightrope-Walking and 'Gender Judo': What Women Have to Do to Get Ahead," *Salon,* March 20, 2014, http://www.salon.com/2014/03/20/tightrope_walking_and_gender_judo_what_women_have_to_do_to_get_ahead/.

40. Aumann, Galinsky, and Matos, "New Male Mystique," 3.

Paternity Leave

1. Abt Associates, "Family Medical Leave in 2012: Executive Summary," updated September 13, 2013, http://www.dol.gov/asp/evaluation/fmla/FMLA-2012-Executive-Summary.pdf.

2. Kenneth Matos and Ellen Galinsky, *2014 National Study of Employers* (New York: Families and Work Institute, 2014), 7.

3. Heather Boushey, Jane Farrell, and John Schmitt, *Job Protection Isn't Enough: Why America Needs Paid Parental Leave* (Washington, DC: Center for American Progress and the Center for Economic and Policy Research, December 2013), 2.

4. Matos and Galinsky, *2014 National Study,* 6.

5. Matos and Galinsky, *2014 National Study,* 6.

6. Matos and Galinsky, *2014 National Study,* 7.

7. Erin M. Rehel, "When Dad Stays Home Too: Paternity Leave, Gender, and Parenting," *Gender and Society* 28 (September 26, 2013): 110, doi:10.1177/0891243213503900.

8. Wendy Wang, Kim Parker, and Paul Taylor, "Breadwinner Moms," *Pew Research Center's Social and Demographic Trends,* 2013, chap. 3.

9. Liza Mundy, "Daddy Track: The Case for Paternity Leave," *Atlantic,* December 22, 2013, http://www.theatlantic.com/magazine/archive/2014/01/the-daddy-track/355746/.

10. Pamela Stone, *Opting Out? Why Women Really Quit Careers and Head Home* (Berkeley, CA: Univ. of California Press, 2007).

Follow the Money

1. Greenberg Quinlan Rosner Research, "The Shriver Report/CAP/AARP Frequency Questionnaire, August 21–September 11, 2013," January 2014, http://cdn.americanprogress.org/wp-content/uploads/2014/01/Women_fq.pdf.

2. Brad Harrington et al., *The New Dad: Take Your Leave: Perspectives on Paternity Leave from Fathers, Leading Organizations, and Global Policies* (Boston: Boston College Center for Work and Family, 2014), 6.

3. National Partnership for Women and Families, "New Poll Shows Bipartisan Voter Mandate for Family-Friendly Workplace Policies," December 3, 2012, http://www.nationalpartnership.org/news-room/press-releases/new-poll-shows-bipartisan-mandate.html.

4. Kenneth Matos and Ellen Galinsky, *2014 National Study of Employers* (New York: Families and Work Institute, 2014), 7.

5. Keith Cunningham-Parmeter, "Father Time: Flexible Work Arrangements and the Law Firm's Failure of the Family," *Stanford Law Review,* April 2001. http://www.highbeam.com/doc/1G1-75092113.html.

6. "Paid Family Leave," State of California Employment Development Department, http://www.edd.ca.gov/disability/paid_family_leave.htm.

7. National Conference of State Legislatures, "State Family and Medical Leave Laws," http://www.ncsl.org/research/labor-and-employment/state-family-and-medical-leave-laws.aspx.

8. Eileen Appelbaum and Ruth Milkman, *Leaves That Pay: Employer and Worker Experiences with Paid Family Leave in California* (New York: Center for Economic and Policy Research, 2011), 2.

9. Barack Obama, "Weekly Address," June 21, 2014.

10. The White House, Office of the Press Secretary, "FACT SHEET: White House Unveils New Steps to Strengthen Working Families Across America," January 14, 2015, http://www.whitehouse.gov/the-press-office/2015/01/14/fact-sheet-white-house-unveils-new-steps-strengthen-working-families-acr.

11. Lydia Wheeler, "Dems' Next Big Issue," *The Hill,* January 13, 2015, http://thehill.com/regulation/business/229292-dems-next-big-issue.

12. Joint Economic Committee Majority Staff, *Paid Family Leave at Fortune 100 Companies: A Basic Standard, but Still Not the Gold Standard* (Washington, DC: Joint Economic Committee, 2008), 11.

13. Ta-Nehisi Coates conversation with Liza Mundy, "The Daddy Track: The Case for Paternity Leave," 59:20, posted by "The Atlantic LIVE," February 18, 2014, http://www.theatlantic.com/live/events/daddy-track/2014/.

14. "H.R.3712: Family and Medical Insurance Leave Act of 2013," U.S. Government Printing Office, 113th Congress, https://www.congress.gov/bill/113th-congress/house-bill/3712/text.

15. Jane Farrell and Sarah Jane Glynn, "The FAMILY Act: Facts and Frequently Asked Questions," *Center for American Progress,* December 12, 2013, http://www

.americanprogress.org/issues/labor/report/2013/12/12/81037/the-family-act-facts
-and-frequently-asked-questions/.

16. "Twentieth Anniversary of the Family and Medical Leave Act," U.S. Department of Labor, http://www.dol.gov/dol/media/webcast/20130205-fmla/.

17. Kirsten Gillibrand, "Paid Family Leave for All, Right Now," *New York Daily News,* January 15, 2014, http://www.nydailynews.com/opinion/paid-family-leave-article -1.1579831.

18. Newsweek Staff, "The Argument Against Paid Family Leave," *Newsweek,* August 4, 2009, http://www.newsweek.com/argument-against-paid-family-leave-78741.

19. Newsweek Staff, "Argument Against Paid Family Leave."

20. OECD Week 2012, Gender Equality in Education, Employment and Entrepreneurship: Final Report to the MCM 2012, May 23–24, 2012, http://www.oecd.org/ social/family/50423364.pdf.

21. European Commission, "More Women in Senior Positions: Key to Economic Stability and Growth, January 2010, http://ec.europa.eu/danmark/documents/alle_ emner/beskaeftigelse/more_women_in_senior_positions.pdf.

22. "Congress Contemplates Major Changes in Employment Law," *Portland Business Journal,* September 2007.

23. U.S. Chamber of Commerce, "Complaint for Declarative, Injunctive and Other Relief," June 26, 2000, https://www.uschamber.com/sites/default/files/legacy/issues/ labor/files/lpainc.v.herman.pdf.

24. Cali Williams Yost, "Three Reasons Why Card-Carrying Capitalists Should Support Paid Family Leave," *Forbes,* May 23, 2012, http://www.forbes.com/sites/ work-in-progress/2012/05/23/3-reasons-why-card-carrying-capitalists-should -support-paid-family-leave/.

25. Brigid Schulte, "States Make Moves Toward Paid Family Leave," *Washington Post,* December 29, 2013, http://www.washingtonpost.com/local/states-make- moves-toward-paid-family-leave/2013/12/29/568691ee-6297-11e3-a373-0f9f2d1c 2b61_story.html.

Paid Family Leave

1. Brad Harrington, Fred Van Deusen, and Beth Humberd, *The New Dad: Caring, Committed and Conflicted* (Boston: Boston College Center for Work and Family, 2011), 26.

2. Tom Nides, "Paid Family Leave Law Long Overdue," *Huffington Post,* January 1, 2014, http://www.huffingtonpost.com/tom-nides/paid-family-leave-law-lon_b_4654839.html.

3. Cali Williams Yost, "Three Reasons Why Card-Carrying Capitalists Should Support Paid Family Leave," *Forbes,* May 23, 2012, http://www.forbes.com/sites/ work-in-progress/2012/05/23/3-reasons-why-card-carrying-capitalists-should -support-paid-family-leave/.

4. Heather Boushey, Jane Farrell, and John Schmitt, *Job Protection Isn't Enough: Why America Needs Paid Parental Leave* (Washington, DC: Center for American Progress and the Center for Economic and Policy Research, December 2013), 3.

5. Boushey, Farrell, and Schmitt, *Job Protection*, 16.

6. Eileen Appelbaum and Ruth Milkman, "Employer and Worker Experiences with Paid Family Leave in California," *Monthly Review* (2011), http://mrzine.monthlyreview.org/2011/am130111.html.

7. Sharon Lerner, "Is Paid Family Leave Bad for Business?" *CNN,* June 23, 2014, http://www.cnn.com/2014/06/18/opinion/lerner-paid-family-leave/.

8. Linda Houser and Thomas P. Vartanian, *Pay Matters: The Positive Economic Impacts of Paid Family Leave for Families, Businesses and the Public* (New Brunswick, NJ: Center for Women and Work, 2012). "CWW's Study Finds Paid Family Leave Leads to Positive Economic Outcomes," Rutgers, January 19, 2012, http://smlr.rutgers.edu/news-events/cwws-study-finds-paid-family-leave-leads-positive-economic-outcomes.

9. National Science Board, *Science and Engineering Indicators 2014* (Arlington, VA: National Science Foundation, 2014), http://www.nsf.gov/statistics/seind14/content/etc/nsb1401.pdf, 7–23.

10. "CNN Town Hall: Hillary Clinton's Hard Choices," CNN Transcripts, June 17, 2014, http://www.cnn.com/TRANSCRIPTS/1406/17/se.01.html.

11. "Parents Caring for Children: The United States Lags Far Behind," *World Policy Forum,* http://worldpolicyforum.org/press/english/WORLD%20Fact%20Sheet%2015%20United%20States%20English.pdf?8328a6.

12. "Status of Ratification Interactive Dashboard," United Nations Office of the High Commissioner for Human Rights, http://indicators.ohchr.org/.

13. "Where Do Fathers Get More Leave?" International Labor Organization, http://www.ilo.org/global/about-the-ilo/multimedia/maps-and-charts/WCMS_241699/lang—en/index.htm.

14. Laura Addati, Naomi Cassirer, and Katherine Gilchrist, *Maternity and Paternity at Work: Law and Practice Across the World* (Geneva: International Labour Organization, 2014), 51.

15. Addati, Cassirer, and Gilchrist, *Maternity and Paternity,* 52.

How to Cover Family Leave by Lowering Taxes

1. Ashlea Ebeling, "New Healthcare Flexible Spending Account Rules for 2013, Use-It-or-Lose-It Still Undecided," *Forbes,* November 16, 2012, http://www.forbes.com/sites/ashleaebeling/2012/11/16/new-healthcare-flexible-spending-account-rules-for-2013-use-it-or-lose-it-still-undecided/.

The Stigma That Makes Men Give Up Billions

1. Paul Taylor et al., "The New American Father," *Pew Research Center's Social and Demographic Trends,* 2013.

2. Laurie A. Rudman and Kris Mescher, "Penalizing Men Who Request a Family Leave: Is Flexibility a Femininity Stigma?" *Journal of Social Issues* 69/2 (2013), doi:10.1111/josi.12017.

3. Scott Coltrane et al., "Fathers and the Flexibility Stigma," *Journal of Social Issues* 69/2 (2013), doi:10.1111/josi.12015.

4. Joseph A. Vandello et al., "When Equal Isn't Really Equal: The Masculine Dilemma of Seeking Work Place Flexibility," *Journal of Social Issues* 69/2 (2013), doi:10.1111/josi.12016.

5. Jennifer L. Berdahl and Sue H. Moon, "Workplace Mistreatment of Middle-Class Workers Based on Sex, Parenthood, and Caregiving," *Journal of Social Issues* 69/2 (2013), doi:10.1111/josi.12018.

6. CBC Community Team, "Caregiving Fathers Stigmatized at Work, Says U of T Study," *CBC*, June 19, 2013, http://www.cbc.ca/newsblogs/yourcommunity/2013/06/fathers-who-prioritize-family-stigmatized-at-work-uoft.html.

7. William H. Rehnquist, Supreme Court opinion, *Nevada Department of Human Resources et al. v Hibbs et al.* (2003), http://caselaw.lp.findlaw.com/scripts/getcase.pl?court=US&vol=000&invol=01-1368.

8. Boris Groysberg and Robin Abrahams, "Manage Your Work, Manage Your Life," *Harvard Business Review*, March 2014, 61.

9. Groysberg and Abrahams, "Manage Your Work," 61.

10. Groysberg and Abrahams, "Manage Your Work," 66.

In Search of Neanderthals

1. Josh Levs, "Open Letter to Boomer & Carton and Mike Francesa, Who Slammed Paternity Leave and Daniel Murphy for Taking It," *levsnews*, April 3, 2014, http://joshlevs.tumblr.com/post/81584314470/open-letter-to-boomer-carton-and-mike-francesa.

2. "Boomer Esiason Apologizes for Comments on Murphy's Paternity Leave," *WFAN*, April 4, 2014, http://newyork.cbslocal.com/2014/04/04/boomer-esiason-apologizes-for-insensitive-comments-on-murphys-paternity-leave/.

3. Jessica Grose, "The Lesson from Baseball's Paternity-Leave Controversy: Paternity Leave Is Not Controversial, *Slate*, April 7, 2014, http://www.slate.com/blogs/xx_factor/2014/04/07/mlb_paternity_leave_controversy_a_happy_ending_to_the_boomer_esiason_flap.html.

4. Adam Rubin, "Daniel Murphy: Right to Take Leave," *ESPN*, April 4, 2014, http://espn.go.com/new-york/mlb/story/_/id/10721495/daniel-murphy-new-york-mets-deflects-criticism-taking-paternity-leave.

5. Scott Behson, "The Good News from the Daniel Murphy Paternity-Leave Uproar," *Wall Street Journal*, April 4, 2014, http://blogs.wsj.com/atwork/2014/04/04/the-good-news-from-the-daniel-murphy-paternity-leave-kerfuffle/.

6. Anthony DiComo, "Murphy Returns to Mets After Paternity Leave," *MLB.com*, April 3, 2014, http://www.mets.mlb.com/news/article/70812196/murphy-returns-to-mets-after-paternity-leave.

7. TMZ Staff, "Daniel Murphy Support from Mets Teammate: 'Family Should Come First,'" *TMZ*, April 5, 2014, http://www.tmz.com/2014/04/05/daniel-murphy-josh-satin-ny-mets-paternity-support/.

Male Privilege, Female Gatekeeping, and the Bonus Temptation

1. Keith Cunningham-Parmeter, "Men at Work, Fathers at Home: Uncovering the Masculine Face of Caregiver Discrimination," *Columbia Journal of Gender and Law* 24 (2013): 255–56, http://ssrn.com/abstract=2351545.
2. Richard Dorment, "Why Men Still Can't Have It All," *Esquire,* June/July 2013, http://www.esquire.com/features/why-men-still-cant-have-it-all-0613.
3. Rebecca Greenfield, "Why Sheryl Sandberg's Husband Can't Have It All," *The Wire,* May 28, 2013, http://www.thewire.com/business/2013/05/sheryl-sandbergs -husband-lean-in/65653/.
4. Sheryl Sandberg, *Lean In: Women, Work, and the Will to Lead* (New York: Knopf, 2013), 108.
5. Tom Stocky, Facebook post, July 7, 2013, https://www.facebook.com/tstocky/ posts/996111776858.
6. Stocky, Facebook.

Flexibility

1. Council of Economic Advisers, "Work-Life Balance and the Economics of Work-place Flexibility," June 2014, http://www.whitehouse.gov/sites/default/files/docs/ updated_workplace_flex_report_final_0.pdf.
2. Kenneth Matos and Ellen Galinsky, *2012 National Study of Employers* (New York: Families and Work Institute, 2012), 3.
3. Brad Harrington, Fred Van Deusen, and Beth Humberd, *The New Dad: Caring, Committed and Conflicted* (Boston: Boston College Center for Work and Family, 2011), 15.
4. Council of Economic Advisers, "Nine Facts About American Families and Work," June 2014, http://www.whitehouse.gov/sites/default/files/docs/nine_facts_about _family_and_work_real_final.pdf.
5. Lisa Belkin, "Marissa Mayer's Work-from-Home-Ban Is the Exact Oppo-site of What CEOs Should Be Doing," *Huffington Post,* April 25, 2013, http:// www.huffingtonpost.com/lisa-belkin/marissa-mayer-work-from-home-yahoo -rule_b_2750256.html.
6. Jenna Goudreau, "Back to the Stone Age? New Yahoo CEO Marissa Mayer Bans Working from Home," *Forbes,* February 25, 2013, http://www.forbes.com/sites/ jennagoudreau/2013/02/25/back-to-the-stone-age-new-yahoo-ceo-marissa-mayer -bans-working-from-home/.
7. Suzanne Lucas, "Top 9 HR Fails of 2013," *Inc.,* December 3, 2013, http://www.inc .com/suzanne-lucas/top-hr-fails-of-2013.html.
8. Drew Hendricks, "Five Ways Telecommuting Saves Employers Money," *Entrepreneur,* July 14, 2014, http://www.entrepreneur.com/article/235285.
9. "Costs and Benefits: Advantages of Telecommuting for Companies," *Global Workplace Analytics,* http://www.globalworkplaceanalytics.com/resources/costs -benefits.

10. "The Survey: Why Men Still Can't Have It All," *Esquire,* May 28, 2013, http://www.esquire.com/features/work-life-cant-have-all-survey-0613.
11. Inc., "Let Them Wear Pajamas," April 2013, p. 32, http://www.incmagazine-digital.com/incmagazine/201304/?pg=34#pg34.
12. Cecilia Elena Rouse, "Work-Life Programs: Attracting, Retaining and Empowering the Federal Workforce," May 4, 2010, http://www.whitehouse.gov/administration/eop/cea/speeches-testimony/work-life-programs.
13. Council of Economic Advisers, "Nine Facts."
14. "How'd He Do It? Mom Corps Success Story—Scott Richey," *Mom Corps Blog,* November 12, 2013, The Mom Corps Blog, "How'd He Do It? Mom Corps Success Story—Scott Richey," November 12, 2013, http://www.momcorps.com/news-blog/blog/blog/2013/11/12/how%27d-he-do-it-mom-corps-success-story---scott-richey.
15. Matos and Galinsky, *2012 National Study, 3.*

How a Bus Could Solve a Parenting Crisis

1. Larry Copeland, "Americans' Commutes Aren't Getting Longer," *USA Today,* March 5, 2013, http://www.usatoday.com/story/news/nation/2013/03/05/americans-commutes-not-getting-longer/1963409/.
2. Annie Lowrey, "Your Commute Is Killing You: Long Commutes Cause Obesity, Neck Pain, Loneliness, Divorce, Stress, and Insomnia," *Slate,* May 26, 2011, http://www.slate.com/articles/business/moneybox/2011/05/your_commute_is_killing_you.html.

In Need of Champions

1. Sarah Jane Glynn, "The Family and Medical Leave Act at 20: Still Necessary, Still Not Enough," *Atlantic,* February 5, 2013, http://www.theatlantic.com/sexes/archive/2013/02/the-family-and-medical-leave-act-at-20-still-necessary-still-not-enough/272605/.
2. Christopher J. Lyons and Becky Pettit, "Compounded Disadvantage: Race, Incarceration, and Wage Growth," *Social Problems* 58/2 (May 2011): 257–80, http://www.jstor.org/stable/10.1525/sp.2011.58.2.257.
3. "Fact Sheet: President Obama's Plan for Early Education for All Americans," *The White House,* February 13, 2013.
4. Bryce Covert, "Melissa Harris-Perry on the Politics and Pitfalls of Motherhood in America," *ThinkProgress,* March 30, 2014 http://thinkprogress.org/economy/2014/03/10/3382941/mhp-motherhood/.
5. Jory John, ed., *Thanks and Have Fun Running the Country: Kids' Letters to President Obama* (San Francisco: McSweeney's, 2009), 826 National, "Writing Gallery," http://www.826national.org/writing-gallery/140/letters-to-president-obama.

The "Doofus Dad" Obsession Must End

1. Josh Levs, "No More Dumb Old Dad: Changing the Bumbling Father Stereo-type," *CNN,* June 6, 2012, http://www.cnn.com/2012/06/12/living/dumb-dad-stereotype/.

2. David A. Holland, "Madison Avenue's Go-to Guy—The Clueless Husband/Father," *Blather. Wince. Repeat.,* July 10, 2011, https://web.archive.org/web/20120817061412/http://blatherwincerepeat.com/?p=3224.

3. Chris Routly, "We're Dads, Huggies. Not Dummies," March 2012, http://www.change.org/p/we-re-dads-huggies-not-dummies.

4. NYC Dads Group, "Raising the Bar for Dads in Advertising," May 10, 2012, http://www.nycdadsgroup.com/2012/05/over-years-weve-been-accused-of-not.html.

5. PR Newswire, "Dove Men+Care Launches 'Real Strength' Campaign on Sports' Biggest Stage to Celebrate the Caring Side of Modern Men," January 20, 2015, http://www.prnewswire.com/news-releases/dove-mencare-launches-real-strength-campaign-on-sports-biggest-stage-to-celebrate-the-caring-side-of-modern-men-300022814.html.

6. "2012 Cone Year of the Dad Trend Tracker," *Cone Communications,* 2012.

7. Stephanie Azzarone, "Dads Are 'Making Inroads,' but Moms Still 'Rule the Roost,'" *Child's Play Communications,* http://www.childsplaypr.com/blog/dads-making-inroads-moms-still-rule-roost/.

8. Zach Rosenberg, "Observations on Dad-Bias in 140 Commercials from 2013," http://www.8bitdad.com/2014/01/17/dad-bias-in-2013-commercials-17917/#sthash.iw4tYIzM.dpuf.

9. Josh Levs, "Amid Fury, Clorox Pulls Post Insulting New Dads," *CNN,* June 27, 2013, http://www.cnn.com/2013/06/27/living/cnn-parents-dads-clorox/.

10. Ralph LaRossa, Charles Jaret, Malati Gadgil, and G. Robert Wynn, "The Chang-ing Culture of Fatherhood in Comic-Strip Families: A Six-Decade Analysis," *Journal of Marriage and Family* 62/2 (May 2000): 375–87, http://www.jstor.org/stable/1566746.

11. Levs, "No More Dumb Old Dad."

Media and the Fear of Men

1. Administration on Children, Youth, and Families, *Child Maltreatment 2012* (Wash-ington, DC: U.S. Department of Health and Human Services, 2012), 61.

2. Julia Whealin and Erin Barnett, "Child Sexual Abuse," National Center for PTSD, U.S. Department of Veterans Affairs, http://www.ptsd.va.gov/professional/trauma/other/child_sexual_abuse.asp.

3. Julia Hislop, "Female Sex Offenders Are Often Overlooked," *New York Times,* February 21, 2013, http://www.nytimes.com/roomfordebate/2013/02/20/too-many-restrictions-on-sex-offenders-or-too-few/female-sex-offenders-are-often-overlooked.

4. S. J. Dallam and J. L. Silberg, "Myths That Place Children at Risk During Custody Disputes," *Sexual Assault Report* 9/3 (January/February 2006): 33–47.

5. Lenore Skenazy, "Bad Advice: 'If You Get Lost, Look for a Mommy'," *ParentDish,* December 7, 2010.

6. Tom Stocky, Facebook post, July 7, 2013, https://www.facebook.com/tstocky/posts/996111776858.

The Truth About Fatherlessness

1. "America's Children: Key National Indicators of Well-Being, 2013," *Forum on Child and Family Statistics,* http://www.childstats.gov/americaschildren13/famsoc1.asp.

2. Isabel Sawhill and Joanna Venator, "Families Adrift: Is Unwed Childbearing the New Norm?" Brookings Institution Social Mobility Memos, October 2013, http://www.brookings.edu/blogs/social-mobility-memos/posts/2014/10/13-unwed-childbearing-new-norm-sawhill.

3. Sally C. Curtin, Stephanie J. Ventura, and Gladys M. Martinez, "Recent Declines in Nonmarital Childbearing in the United States," U.S. Centers for Disease Control, National Center for Health Statistics Data Brief No. 162, August 2014, http://www.cdc.gov/nchs/data/databriefs/db162.pdf.

4. Jo Jones and William D. Mosher, "Fathers' Involvement with Their Children: United States, 2006–2010," *National Health Statistics Reports* 71 (2013): 6, http://www.cdc.gov/nchs/data/nhsr/nhsr071.pdf.

5. National Fatherhood Initiative, "Statistics on the Father Absence Crisis in America," http://www.fatherhood.org/father-absence-statistics.

6. Dwayne interviewed by Oprah Winfrey, "Why This Father Says He Walked Away from His Family," YouTube video, 4:18, posted by OWN TV, May 4, 2013, https://www.youtube.com/watch?v=YpJ5aKUCFEE.

7. Naomi Cahn and June Carbone, "Just Say No: For White Working-Class Women, It Makes Sense to Stay Single Mothers," *Slate,* April 22, 2014, http://www.slate.com/articles/double_x/doublex/2014/04/white_working_class_women_should_stay_single_mothers_argue_the_authors_of.html.

8. Cahn and Carbone, "Just Say No."

9. Wendy Wang, Kim Parker, and Paul Taylor, "Breadwinner Moms: Mothers Are the Sole or Primary Provider in Four-in-Ten Households with Children; Public Conflicted About the Growing Trend," *Pew Research Center's Social and Demographic Trends,* May 29, 2013, http://www.pewsocialtrends.org/2013/05/29/breadwinner-moms/.

10. "Labor Force Statistics from the Current Population Survey," Bureau of Labor Statistics, 2012, http://www.bls.gov/cps/aa2012/cpsaat11.htm.

11. Thomas S. Dee, "How a Teacher's Gender Affects Boys and Girls," https://cepa.stanford.edu/sites/default/files/ednext20064_68.pdf.

How Black Dads Are Doing Best of All

1. Jo Jones and William D. Mosher, "Fathers' Involvement with Their Children: United States, 2006–2010," *National Health Statistics Reports* 71 (2013), http://www.cdc.gov/nchs/data/nhsr/nhsr071.pdf.
2. Jones and Mosher, "Fathers' Involvement with Their Children."
3. Jonathan Vespa, Jamie M. Lewis, and Rose M. Kreider, *America's Families and Living Arrangements: 2012* (Washington, DC: U.S. Census Bureau, August 2013), 14, http://www.census.gov/prod/2013pubs/p20-570.pdf.
4. Rose M. Kreider and Renee Ellis, *Living Arrangements of Children: 2009* (Washington, DC: U.S. Census Bureau, 2011), http://www.census.gov/prod/2011pubs/p70-126.pdf.
5. Remarks by President Obama on "My Brother's Keeper" Initiative, February 27, 2014.
6. Ta-Nehisi Coates conversation with Liza Mundy, "The Daddy Track: The Case for Paternity Leave," 59:20, posted by "The Atlantic LIVE," February 18, 2014, http://www.theatlantic.com/live/events/daddy-track/2014/.
7. Doyin Richards, "I Have A Dream," *Daddy Doin' Work*, October 15, 2013, http://daddydoinwork.com/dreamin/.

Dads in Prison Open Up

1. Nicholas Kristof, "Inside a Mental Health Hospital Called Jail," *New York Times*, February 8, 2014.
2. Doris J. James and Lauren E. Glaze, "Mental Health Problems of Prison and Jail Inmates," *Bureau of Justice Statistics Special Report* (September 2006), 1, http://www.bjs.gov/content/pub/pdf/mhppji.pdf.
3. Lauren E. Glaze and Laura M. Maruschak, "Parents in Prison and Their Minor Children," *Bureau of Justice Statistics Special Report* (March 30, 2010), 2, http://www.bjs.gov/content/pub/pdf/pptmc.pdf.
4. Glaze and Maruschak, "Parents in Prison," 1.
5. Glaze and Maruschak, "Parents in Prison," 3.

How Military Dads Are Staying Connected

1. "Impacts on Care: Children of Deployed Parents at Increased Risk for Behavioral, Psychological Problems," *VA Research Currents*, February 26, 2014, http://www.research.va.gov/currents/winter2013-14/winter2013-14-28.cfm.
2. *2011 Demographics: Profile of the Military Community* (Washington, DC: Office of the Deputy Under Secretary of Defense, November 2012), vi, http://www.militaryonesource.mil/12038/MOS/Reports/2011_Demographics_Report.pdf.
3. Tova B. Walsh et al., "Fathering After Military Deployment: Parenting Challenges and Goals of Fathers of Young Children," *Health Social Work* (2014), doi: 10.1093/hsw/hlu005.

Courts, Custody, and "Deadbeat Parents"

1. "Getting Custody FAQ," *FindLaw*, http://family.findlaw.com/child-custody/frequently-asked-questions-regarding-custody-of-a-child.html#Q3.

2. David Pisarra, "The 'Y' Factor: Gender Bias, Child Custody and the Great Parenting Myth," *Huffington Post*, March 28, 2011, http://www.huffingtonpost.com/david-t-pisarra/the-y-factor-gender-bias-_b_838631.html.

3. Timothy Grall, *Custodial Mothers and Fathers and Their Child Support* (Washington, DC: U.S. Census Bureau, October 2013), 1, http://www.census.gov/prod/2013pubs/p60-246.pdf.

4. Patricia Brown and Steven T. Cook, "Children's Placement Arrangements in Divorce and Paternity Cases in Wisconsin," *Institute for Research on Poverty*, September 2011, http://www.irp.wisc.edu/research/childsup/cspolicy/pdfs/2009-11/Task4A_CS_09-11_Final_revi2012.pdf.

5. Cathy Meyer, "Dispelling the Myth of Gender Bias in the Family Court System," *Huffington Post*, July 10, 2012, http://www.huffingtonpost.com/cathy-meyer/dispelling-the-myth-of-ge_b_1617115.html.

6. Sally Abrahms, "Custody Lost," http://www.workingmother.com/special-reports/custody-lost.

7. Lisa Belkin, "More Fathers Are Getting Custody in Divorce," *New York Times*, November 17, 2009, http://parenting.blogs.nytimes.com/2009/11/17/more-fathers-getting-custody-in-divorce/?_php=true&_type=blogs&_r=0.

8. S. J. Dallam and J. L. Silberg, "Myths That Place Children at Risk During Custody Disputes," *Sexual Assault Report* 9/3 (January/February 2006): 33–47. S. J. Dallam and J. L. Silberg, "Myths That Place Children at Risk During Custody Litigation," The Leadership Council on Child Abuse and Interpersonal Violence, January/February 2006, http://www.leadershipcouncil.org/1/res/cust_myths.html.

9. "Georgia Deprives Children as Indigent Parents Languish in Debtors' Jail for Inability to Pay Child Support," *Southern Center for Human Rights*, https://www.schr.org/our-work/debtors-prisons/child-support.

10. Elaine Sorensen and Chava Zibman, *Poor Dads Who Don't Pay Child Support: Deadbeats or Disadvantaged?* (Washington, DC: Urban Institute, April 2001), 1.

11. Grall, *Custodial Mothers and Fathers*, 10.

12. Grall, *Custodial Mothers and Fathers*, 11.

13. Linda Laughlin, *Who's Minding the Kids? Child Care Arrangements: Spring 2011* (Washington, DC: U.S. Census Bureau, 2013).

14. Geoff Williams, "What to Do When Your Ex Won't (or Can't) Pay Child Support," *U.S. News and World Report*, November 20, 2013, http://money.usnews.com/money/personal-finance/articles/2013/11/20/what-to-do-when-your-ex-wont-pay-child-support.

Widowers and Motherlessness

1. Gretchen Livingston, "The Rise of Single Fathers: A Ninefold Increase Since 1960," *Pew Research Center's Social and Demographic Trends*, July 2, 2013.

2. United States Census Bureau, Table FG6, "One-Parent Unmarried Family Groups with Own Children/1 Under 18, by Marital Status of the Reference Person: 2013" (Washington, DC., U.S. Census Bureau, 2013), http://www.census.gov/hhes/families/files/cps2013/tabFG6-all_one.xls.

3. Phyllis R. Silverman, "Remembering Fathers Are Also Widowed," *Psychology Today,* July 25, 2010, http://www.psychologytoday.com/blog/raising-grieving-children/201007/remembering-fathers-are-also-widowed.

4. United States Census Bureau, Table FG6, "One-Parent Unmarried Family Groups with Own Children/1 Under 18, by Marital Status of the Reference Person: 2013" (Washington, DC., U.S. Census Bureau, 2013), http://www.census.gov/hhes/families/files/cps2013/tabFG6-all_one.xls.

5. "Casualties," CNN.com, http://www.cnn.com/SPECIALS/war.casualties/.

6. Josh Levs, "Georgia Guard Mourns Iraq Losses," *NPR,* August 6, 2005, http://www.npr.org/templates/story/story.php?storyId=4788809.

The Truth About Parents and Sex

1. Elizabeth Bernstein, "How Often Should Married Couples Have Sex? What Happens When He Says 'More' and She Says 'No,'" *Wall Street Journal,* April 22, 2013, http://online.wsj.com/news/articles/SB10001424127887324874204578438713861797052.

2. Amanda Hess, "The *Wall Street Journal*'s Solution to Sexless Marriages: Stereotype All Men and Women," *Slate,* April 24, 2013, http://www.slate.com/blogs/xx_factor/2013/04/24/sexless_marriage_the_wall_street_journal_s_gender_stereotyping_fails_to.html.

3. Lori Gottlieb, "Does a More Equal Marriage Mean Less Sex?" *New York Times Magazine,* February 9, 2014, http://www.nytimes.com/2014/02/09/magazine/does-a-more-equal-marriage-mean-less-sex.html.

4. Sabino Kornrich, Julie Brines, and Katrina Leupp, "Egalitarianism, Housework, and Sexual Frequency in Marriage," *American Sociological Review* 78/1 (2013): 26–50, http://asr.sagepub.com/content/78/1/26.full.pdf+html.

5. Isaac Chotiner, "This New York Times Sex Story Has One of the Best 'To Be Sure' Paragraphs Ever," *New Republic,* February 6, 2014, http://www.newrepublic.com/article/116512/new-york-times-story-married-couples-and-sex.

6. Constance T. Gager, "Who Has the Time? The Relationship Between Household Labor Time and Sexual Frequency," *Journal of Family Issues* 31/2 (February 2010): 135–63, doi: 10.1177/0192513X09348753.

7. Jaesok Son, analysis of the 2012 data in the *General Social Surveys, 1972–2012,* relating to household chores and sex (analysis commissioned by Josh Levs); Tom W. Smith, Peter Marsden, Michael Hout, and Jibum Kim, *General Social Surveys, 1972–2012* (Chicago: National Opinion Research Center).

8. Center for Sexual Health Promotion (Indiana University–Bloomington), "National Survey of Sexual Health and Behaviors," *Journal of Sexual Medicine* 7 Suppl. (October 2010): 269.

9. Center for Sexual Health Promotion, "National Survey," 295.

Body

1. Centers for Disease Control and Prevention, "Insufficient Sleep Is a Public Health Epidemic," http://www.cdc.gov/features/dssleep/.
2. Centers for Disease Control and Prevention, "Insufficient Sleep."
3. Lisa Belkin, "Men Gain Weight During Pregnancy," *New York Times,* June 2, 2009 http://parenting.blogs.nytimes.com/2009/06/02/men-who-swell-with-pregnancy/.
4. Victoria Ward, "New Fathers 'Gain More Than a Stone When Baby Is Born'" *Telegraph,* October 2014, http://www.telegraph.co.uk/health/9332359/New-fathers-gain-more-than -a-stone-when-baby-is-born.html.
5. Rodlescia S. Sneed et al., "Parenthood and Host Resistance to the Common Cold," *Psychosomatic Medicine* 74/6 (2012), doi:10.1097/PSY.0b013e31825941ff.
6. Michael L. Eisenberg et al., "Fatherhood and the Risk of Cardiovascular Mortality in the NIH-AARP Diet and Health Study," *Human Reproduction* (2011), doi:10.1093/humrep/der305.
7. Maria Ramirez, "Well-Being and Being a Dad: UH Study Finds Health Benefits to Engaging with Children," University of Houston, June 5, 2013, http://www.uh.edu/news-events/stories/2013/june/6%205%20FathersDay.php.

Mind

1. Josh Levs, "Victim: 'You Could Feel the Anger in the Room,'" *CNN,* June 23, 2012, http://www.cnn.com/2012/07/23/justice/courtroom-anger-holmes/.
2. Man Therapy, http://www.mantherapy.org.
3. Rick Nauert, "Men's Mental Health Suffers After Divorce," *PsychCentral,* October 1, 2013, http://psychcentral.com/news/2013/10/01/mens-mental-health-suffers -after-divorce/60153.html.
4. "Depression in Men," *National Institute of Mental Health,* http://www.nimh.nih .gov/health/topics/depression/men-and-depression/depression-in-men.shtml.

Spirit

1. Samara Wolpe, "My Story," *Huffington Post,* March 25, 2014, http://www.huffington post.com/samara-wolpe/my-story_3_b_5028017.html.

The Value of Less

1. Josh Levs, "Overscheduled Kids, Anxious Parents," *CNN,* March 10, 2013, http:// www.cnn.com/2013/03/08/living/overscheduled-busy-children/.

Loving Parenthood

1. Oren Miller, "Cancer," *A Blogger and a Father,* June 3, 2014, http://www.bloggerfather .com/2014/06/cancer.html.

Index

About the Author

Josh Levs has spent years reporting for CNN, where his work as a leader of the "Truth Squad"—separating fact from fiction—earned him the nicknames "Truth Seeker in Chief" and "The Explainer." A committed parent of three children, Levs became one of the most prominent voices for fathers as CNN.com's "dad columnist" and "resident dad" on HLN. When his employer refused him fair parental leave to care for his newborn daughter, Levs took legal action and won—earning plaudits from men's and women's groups, and cementing his role as an advocate for modern families. Levs also covers a wide range of topics and was named "one of the most social media–savvy broadcast journalists" by PBS. Prior to CNN, he was a reporter for NPR. Born in Boston, Levs grew up in a suburb of Albany, New York, and graduated from Yale University. His career honors include six Peabody Awards, two Edward R. Murrow Awards, and awards from the National Association of Black Journalists. The Atlanta Press Club named him a Journalist of the Year. Levs lives in Atlanta, Georgia, with his wife and children.